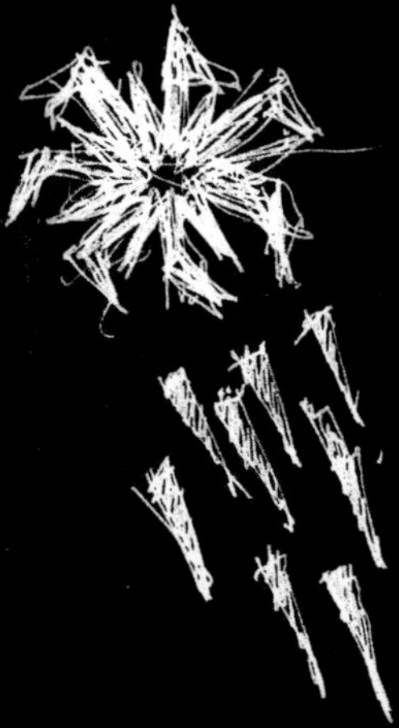

SANCTUARIES

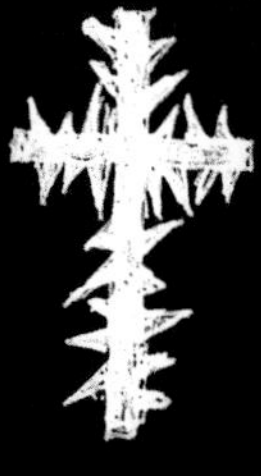

SANCTUARIES

Selections from the John Hejduk Archive at the Canadian Centre for Architecture, Montreal & The Menil Collection, Houston

The Last Works of
JOHN HEJDUK

K. Michael Hays

Whitney Museum of American Art
in association with Harvard Design School
& The Menil Collection
Distributed by Harry N. Abrams, Inc.

DIRECTOR'S FOREWORD

Those of us who were fortunate enough to have known John Hejduk even slightly are grateful for any opportunity to keep his spirit alive. Some fifteen years ago I explored the possibility of acquiring the twenty-foot towers in the present exhibition for another museum, and have remained entranced by his vision ever since. In a society that adulates those who leave large and visible reminders of themselves, Hejduk stood apart. His quiet provocations challenged more prolific peers and inspired a generation of young architects to think in unconventional ways.

At a time when architecture for the most part resists overt allusions to those who commission and inhabit it, Hejduk unabashedly introduced symbolic figuration, playing on biomorphic forms to enliven spaces created for human and animal occupants, as well as for angels and machines.

The sanctuary of the Whitney, completed by Marcel Breuer in 1966, provides a fitting haven for this tribute to Hejduk, which highlights his absorption late in life in the theme of the sanctuary. While Breuer had thought to build a cool fortress for art, safe from the assaults of commerce, Hejduk reveled in the potential of figurative animation to transform the built environment into one symbolically evocative of nature and the divine.

Susan de Menil championed this project from the beginning, and it was Michael Hays, the Whitney's adjunct curator of architecture, who shaped it and the accompanying exhibition at the Whitney. We are grateful to Toshiko Mori, chair of the Department of Architecture of the Harvard University Graduate School of Design, for supporting this publication and the attendant celebration of the life of John Hejduk. Garrett White of our Department of Publications and New Media produced this sensitive publication with the help of managing editor Rachel Wixom, exhibitions and collections management coordinator Meg Calvert, and designer Kim Shkapich.

We are honored to provide this tribute to a great force in American architecture, and look forward to other evaluations of the achievements of this complex but gentle and generous colossus.

Maxwell L. Anderson

Alice Pratt Brown Director
Whitney Museum of American Art

ILLUMINATED PRESENCE

A poem is a poem, a building is a building, architecture is architecture, music is…it's all structure. Essential. I use it as language. Architects are organically responsible today to have their language run parallel with their structure. You know what I'm getting at? The new edge in architecture. I cannot do a building without building a new repertoire of characters of stories of language and it's all parallel. It's not just building per se. It's building worlds. —John Hejduk[1]

John Hejduk, who died on July 3, 2000, was, in a sense, the last architect of the twentieth century and the first architect of the twenty-first. In his work and teaching, he embodied the spirit of architecture at the time of transition from one millennium to the next. In his prolific body of work, in which he chose each medium to suit the particular site and subject matter, he animated life in stillness, measured sounds in silence, and illuminated presence within the void. His projects represent the Before Life, Still Life, and After Life of buildings.

Hejduk was a person of immense and imposing presence, both physically and spiritually. When he spoke, his powerful voice marked by a Bronx accent, everyone listened. He was very much a part of the high-spirited community of New York City architects whose practice and influence expanded to the rest of the world. Yet he always talked about the fragility and delicacy of architecture, and the need for gentleness and love in our daily life and work.

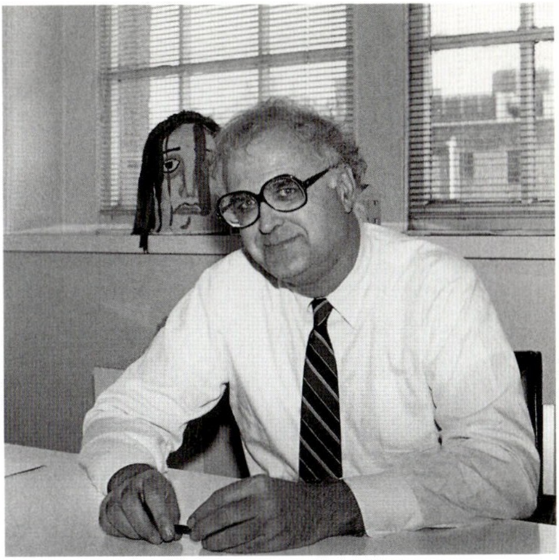

The transition between the millennia represented a precarious threshold. The twentieth century opened with Einstein's theory of relativity and Freud's speculation on the unconscious. Frames of reference and zones of meaning were punctured, and thoughts were no longer able to be contained through rational references to one another. Acknowledgment of the world of relative values and recognition of the power of internal psychic life became the major engines of culture in contemporary society.

John Hejduk's Wall House projects create thresholds between internal and external realms, where boundaries become ambiguous. His Fabrications are characters set in motion to occupy sites and territories that provoke hidden memories of cities such as Prague, Berlin, Vladivostok, and Oslo. In his works, myth is exposed and absorbed into public consciousness. Windows are no longer mere openings in a facade, but take on a de Chiricoesque sense of absence. Walls exude emotive power and buildings gain their own will: his buildings act as witnesses to the history and memory of cities. We even dream with him, about mythical creatures peeking in and out of cracks and crevices. In a singular, monumental effort, John Hejduk dared to expand the boundary of the discipline of architecture by claiming territory within our imagination.

Enclosures, a series of thirty-two drawings represented in its entirety in this catalogue, are allegories of a time that was once safely enclosed, framed, protected, and guarded. John Hejduk believed in the linear nature of time; he existed in the flatness of space. When an angel penetrates a wall and becomes trapped in it, life and death implode at the moment of collision, and space and time fold into infinity. The *Enclosures* bound terrestrial and celestial creatures, mortal and immortal states of being, the struggle between spiritual potency and physical limitation. Ascending and descending bodies float in dense air pierced with interpenetrating light. Visions of depth are expressed in a richly chromatic liquidity—the hue one imagines existing only in paradise or hell. This is the moment when abstract and figurative lose their dialectical relationship; likewise, in his work tectonic rigor and narrative myth inhabit the same plane. In Hejduk's *Enclosures*, Giotto and Piero della Francesca collapse into Barnett Newman through Georges Braque. After decades of exploration of geometry and tectonic principles, the gradual appearance of figures in his work represents the collision of the secular and spiritual worlds. As in Michelangelo's *Last Judgment*, where the artist used human figures to describe architectural alignments, bodies and creatures spatially transform the sectional containers of the *Enclosures*. These works are the Book of Hours of our time—unearthly events inscribed on our souls.

John Hejduk's provocative work carries with it enormous emotive power: the height of exultation is equal to the depth of despair. He prepares us to augment our mental and emotional capacity to withstand perhaps the most horrific visions yet to come, or to witness the most incredible revelatory event, so that we can spiritually survive them. This is not to make us immune to such shocks but rather to draw us into further engagement with all the trials of humanity.

John Hejduk was head of the school of architecture at The Cooper Union for thirty-five years. There he built a sanctuary for the study of architecture and a place for the active exchange of creative thoughts. He nurtured and protected it. Those of us who were fortunate enough to have been his students or friends continue his legacy in many places, aiming to practice and teach with his same generosity of spirit. In the end, it was John Hejduk himself who personified the meaning of sanctuary for many of us. We miss him greatly, but through his work we can continue to enter and inhabit this remarkable place.

Toshiko Mori

Robert P. Hubbard Professor in the Practice of Architecture
Chair, Department of Architecture
Harvard University Graduate School of Design

1. John Hejduk, "The Architect Who Drew Angels," interview by David Shapiro, *Architecture and Urbanism* no. 244 (January 1991), 61.

This is the time for drawing angels. —John Hejduk

■ 2 3 4 5 6 7 8 9 10 11 12 13 14 15 16 17 18 19 20 21 22 23 24 25 26 27 28 29 30 31 32

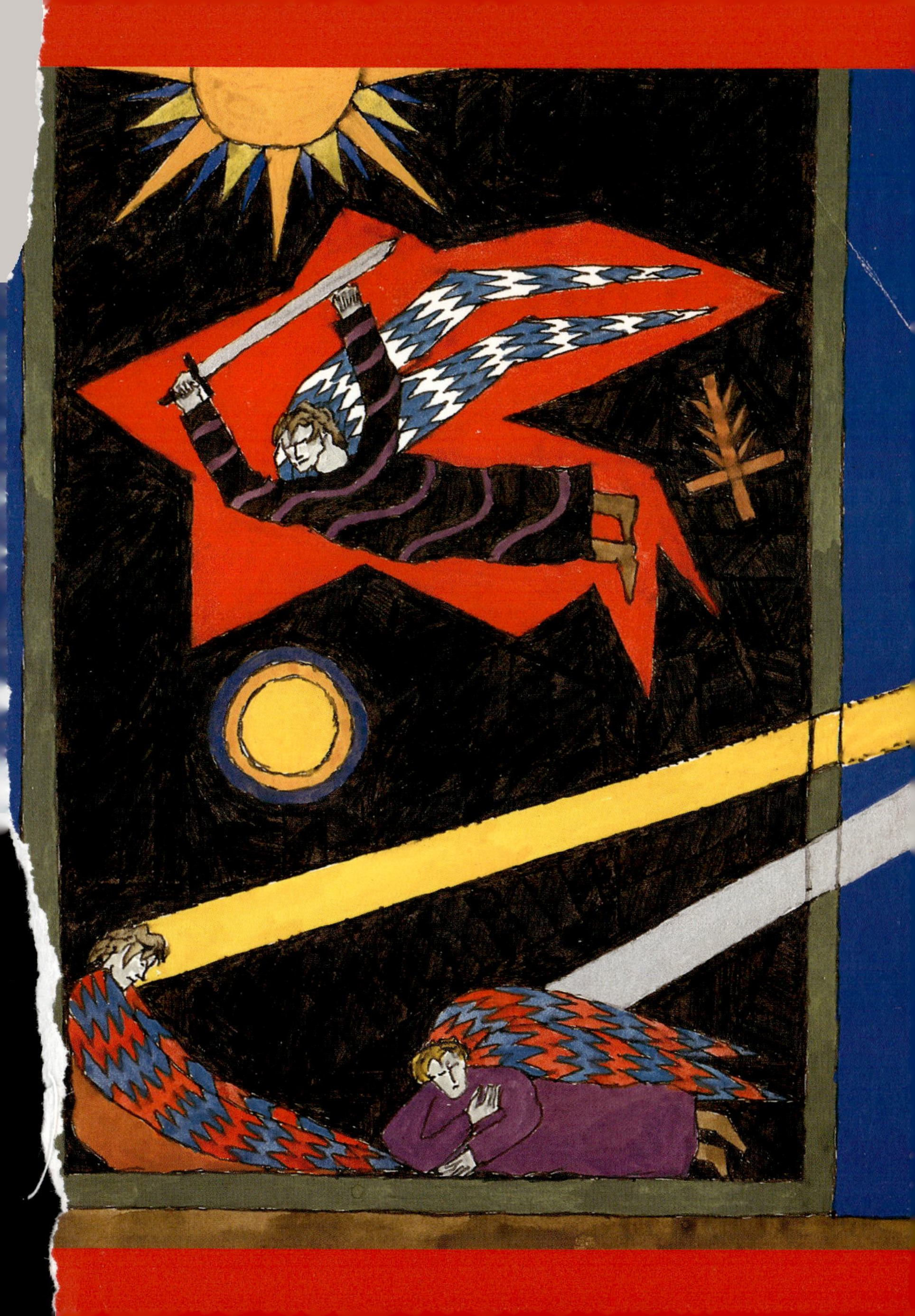

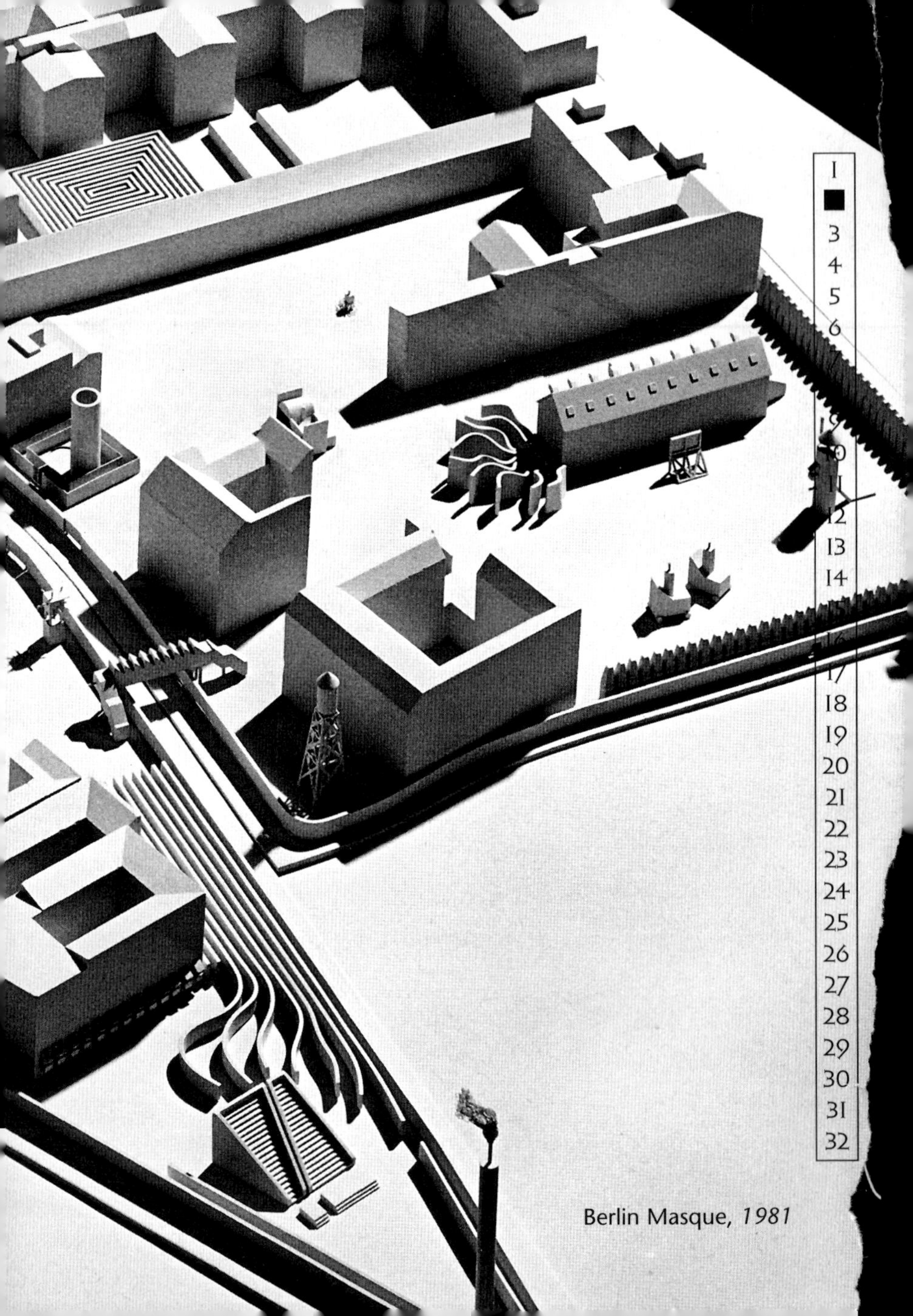

Berlin Masque, *1981*

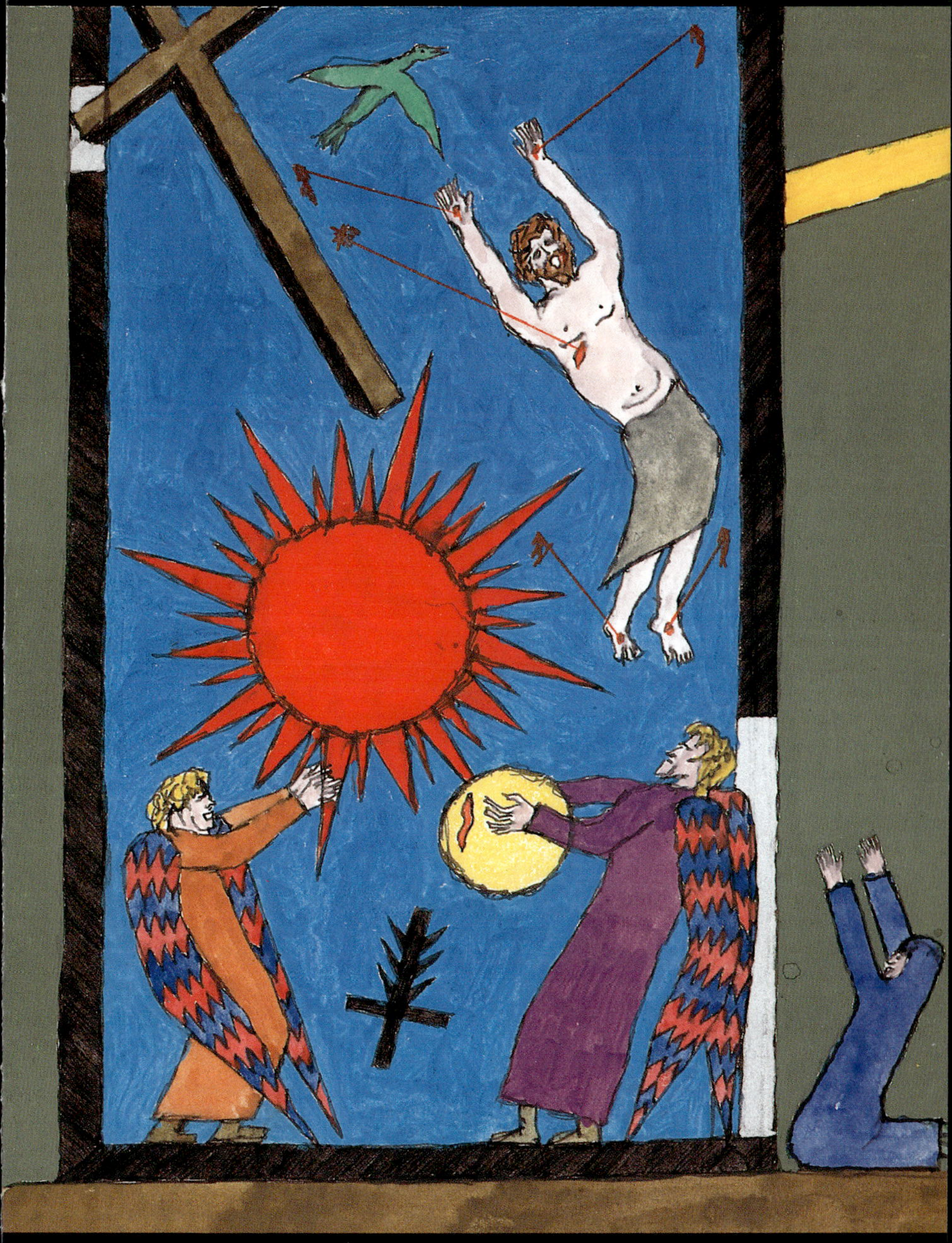

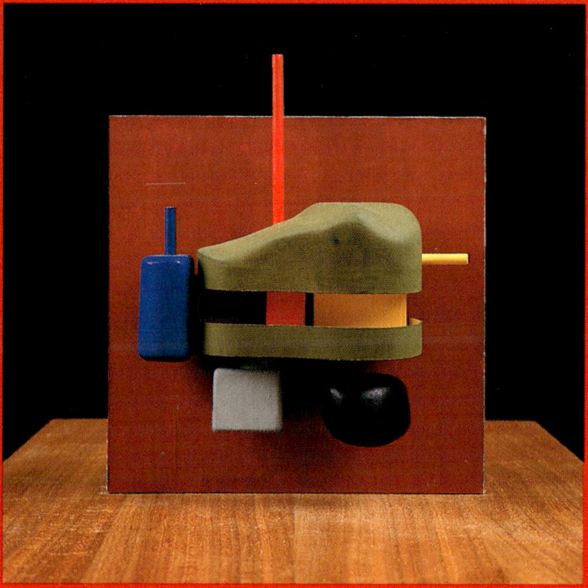

1
2
■
4
5
6
7
8
9
10
11
12
13
14
15
16
17
18
19
20
21
22
23
24
25
26
27
28
29
30
31
32

Wall House 3, *1974*

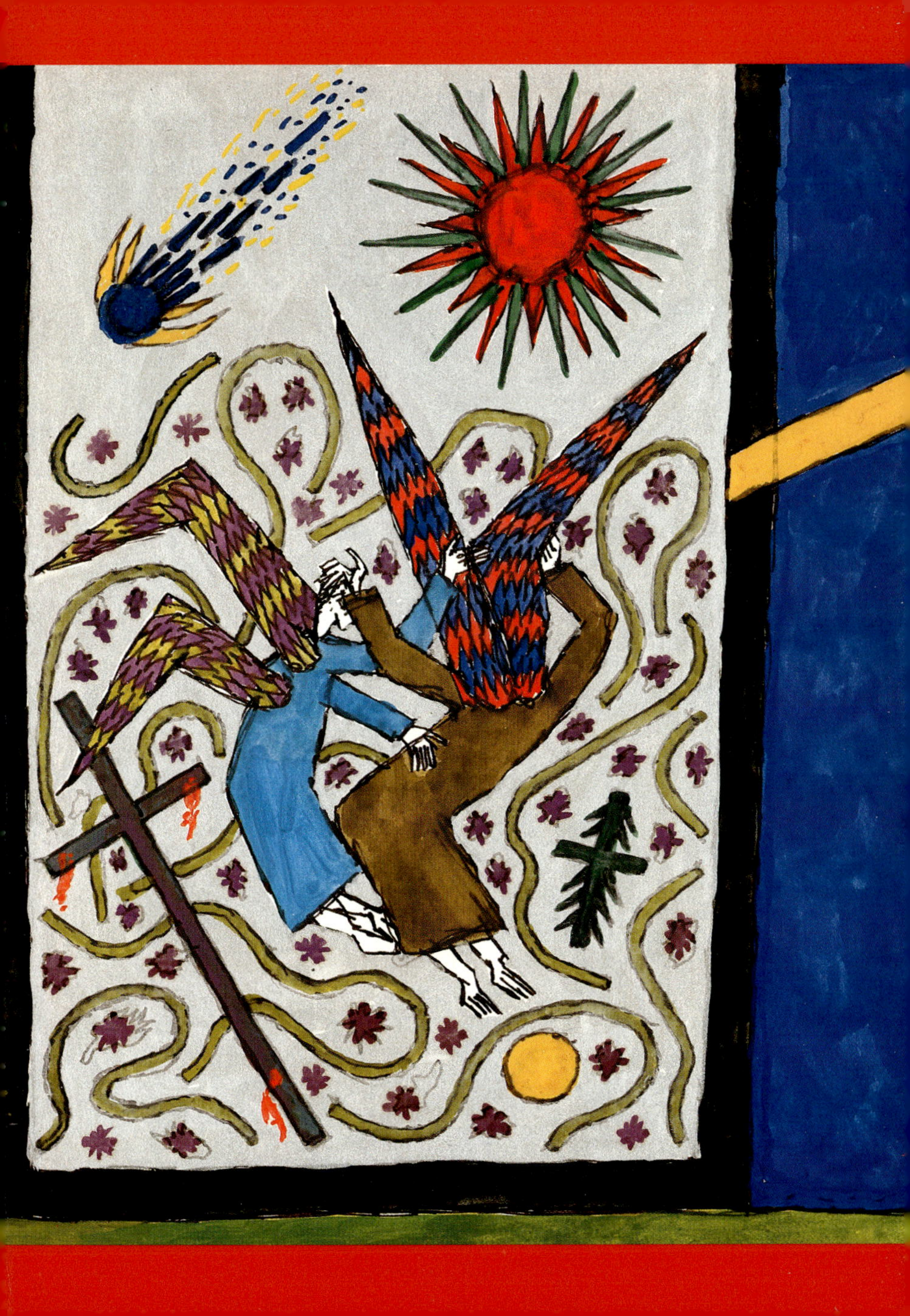

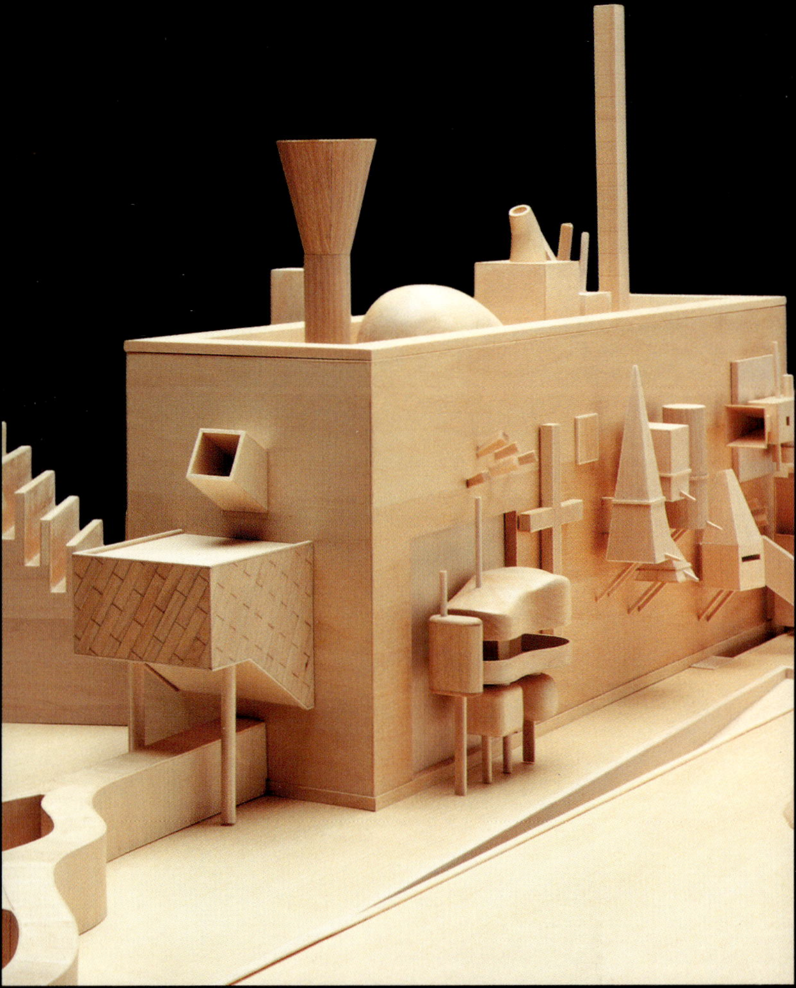

Cathedral, *1996* (detail)

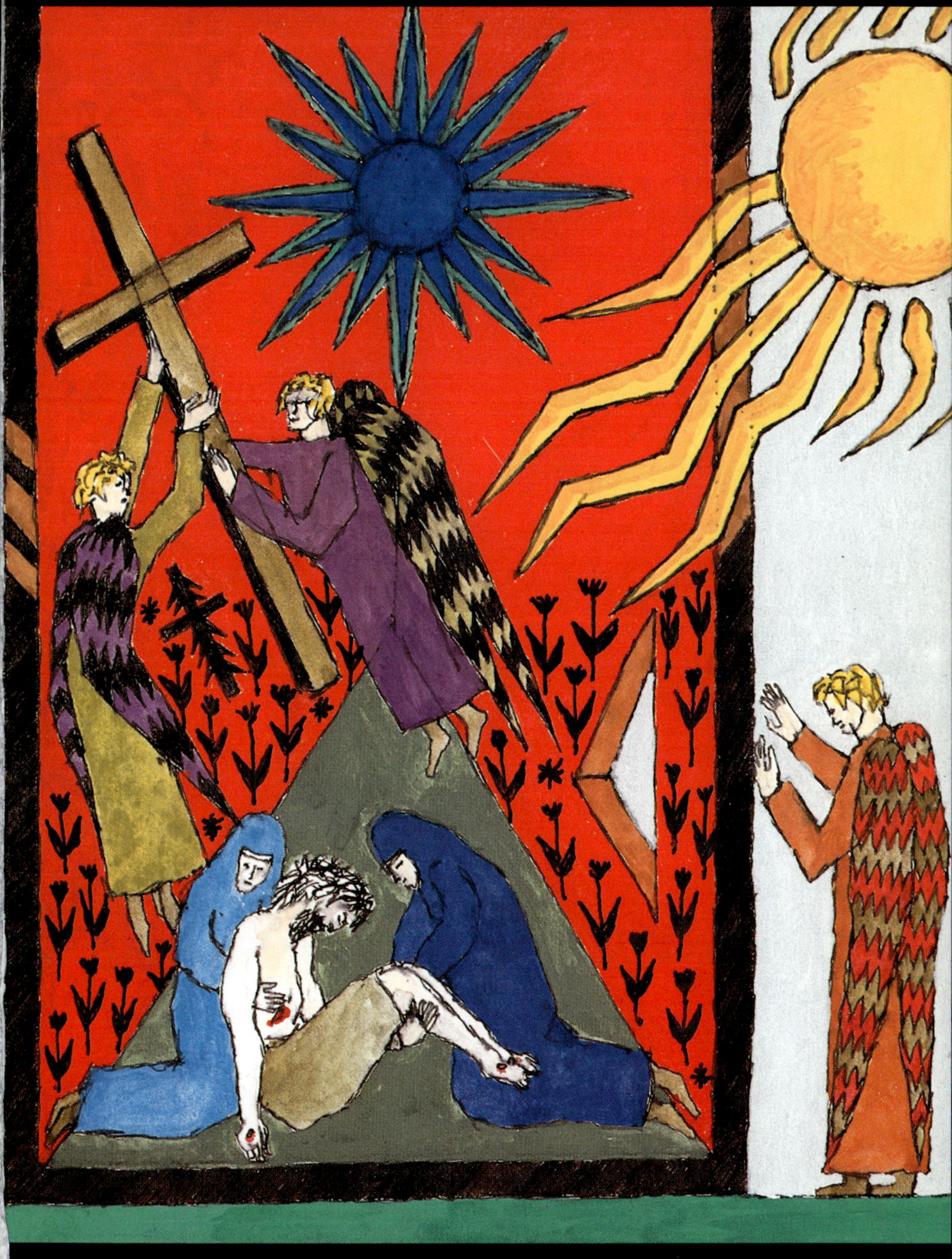

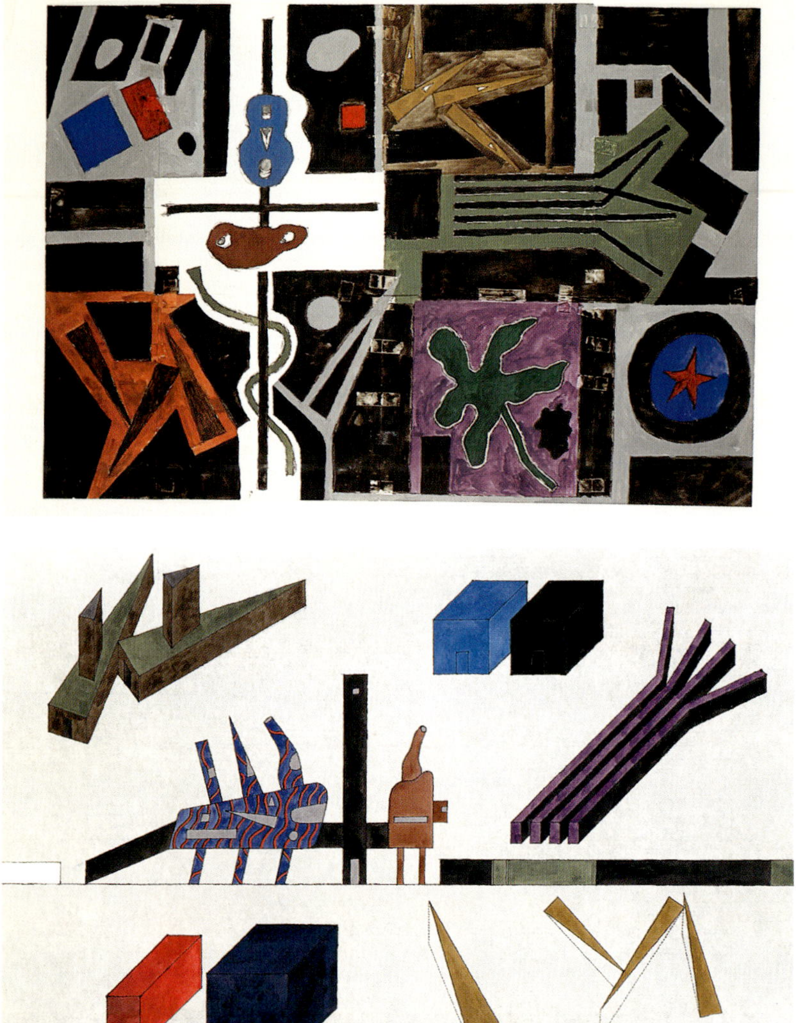

The Red Cube, "Blood from Paul Celan," *1999–2000*

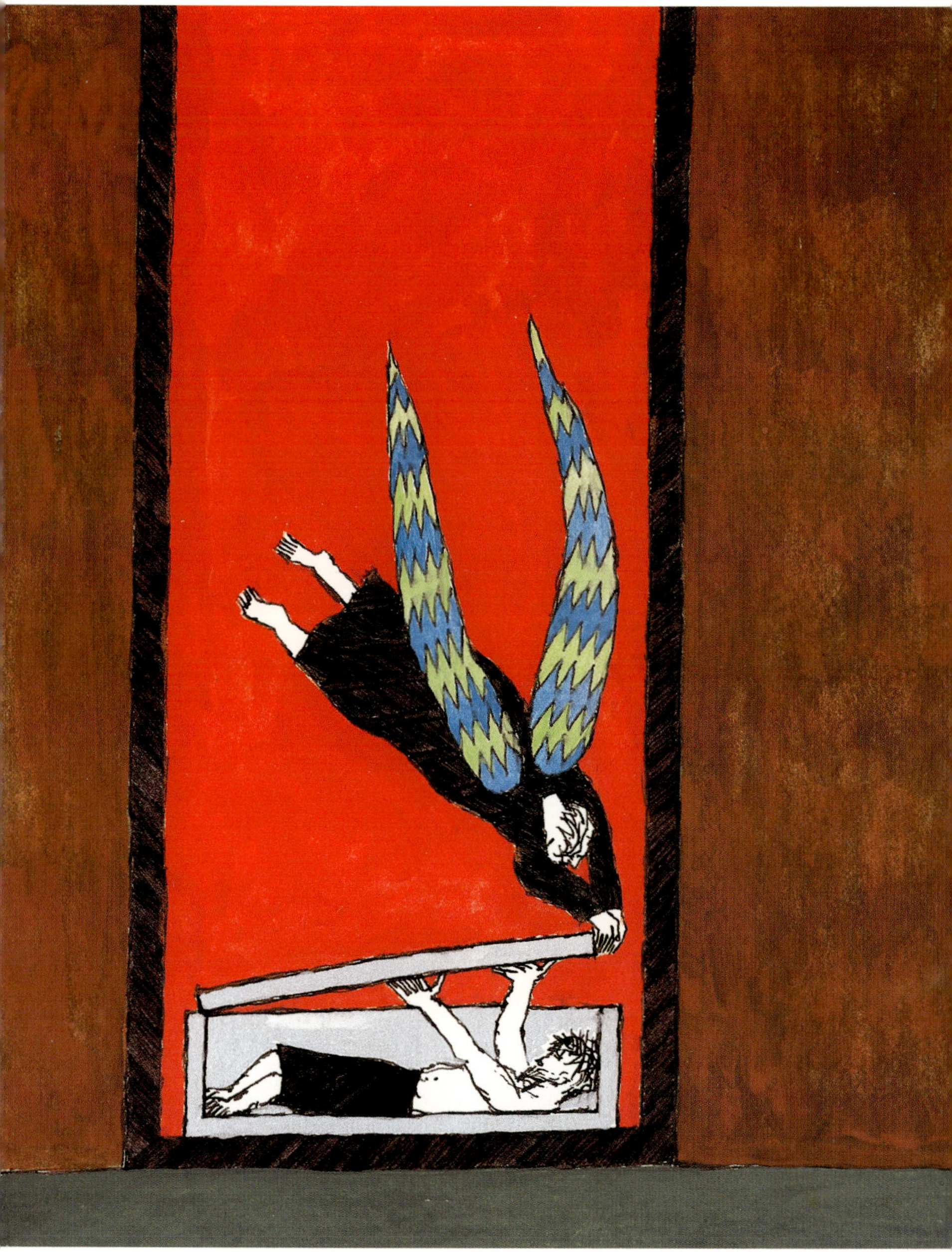

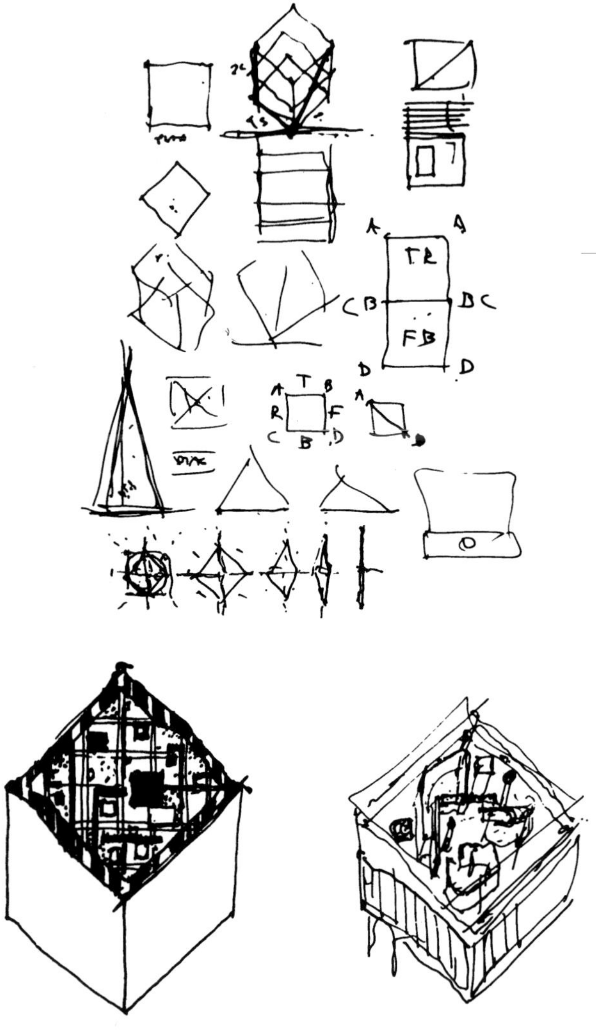

1
2
3
4
5
■
7
8
9
10
11
12
13
14
15
16
17
18
19
20
21
22
23
24
25
26
27
28
29
30
31
32

Diamond Museum C, *1962–67*

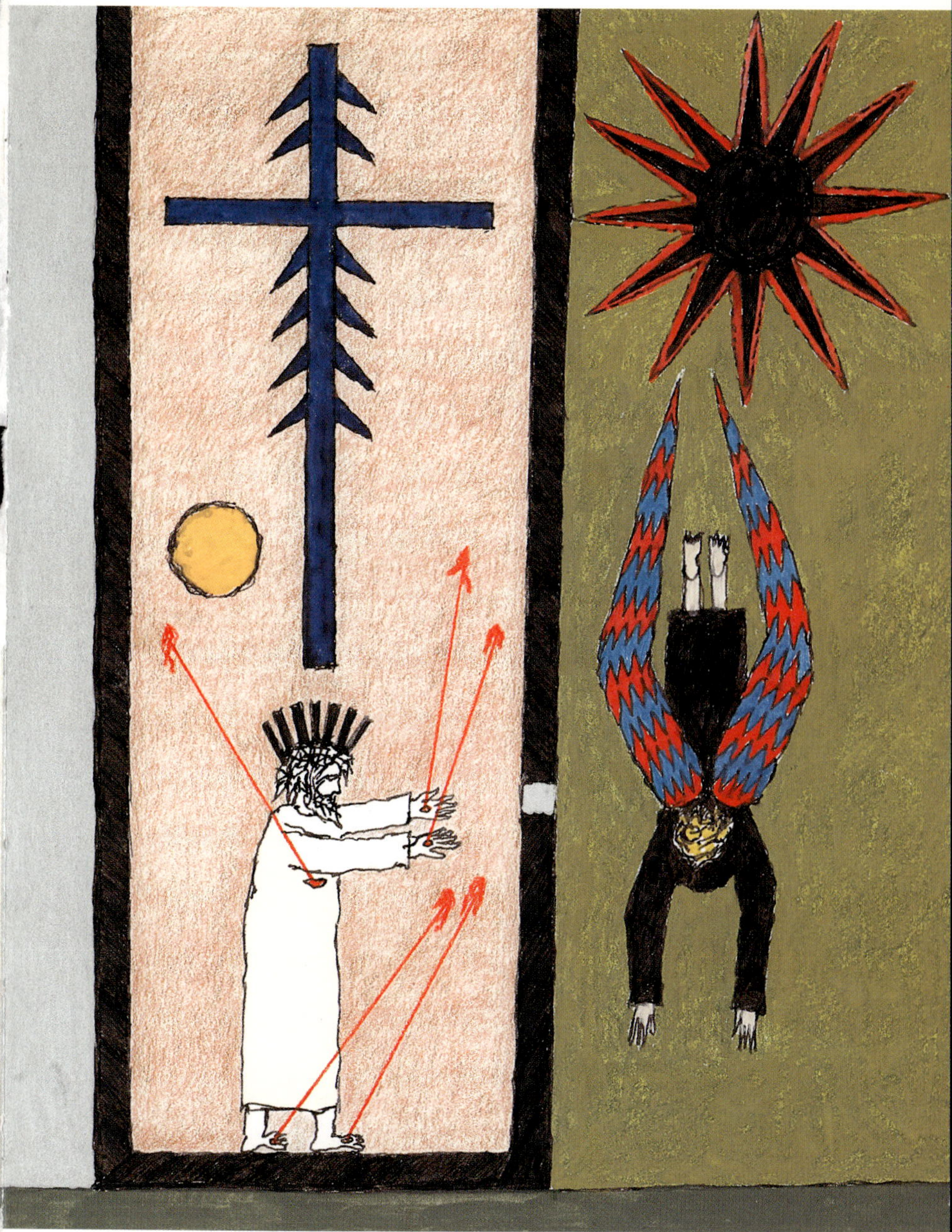

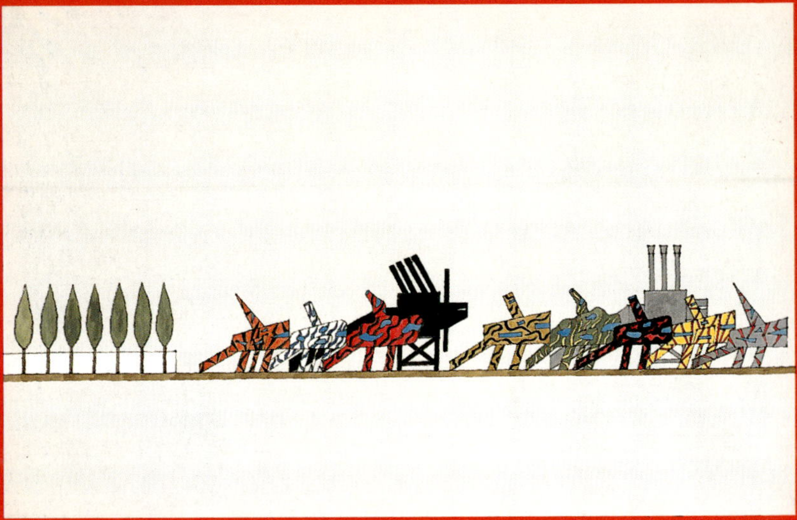

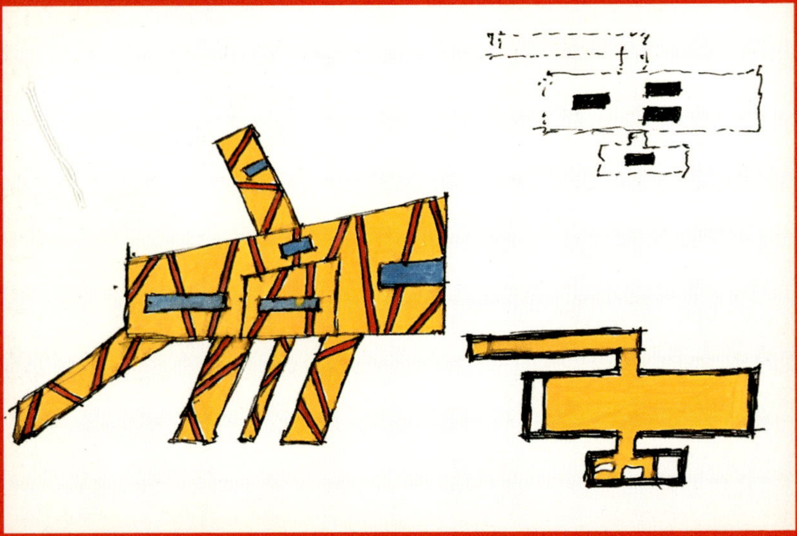

Museum for War and Peace, *1999–2000*

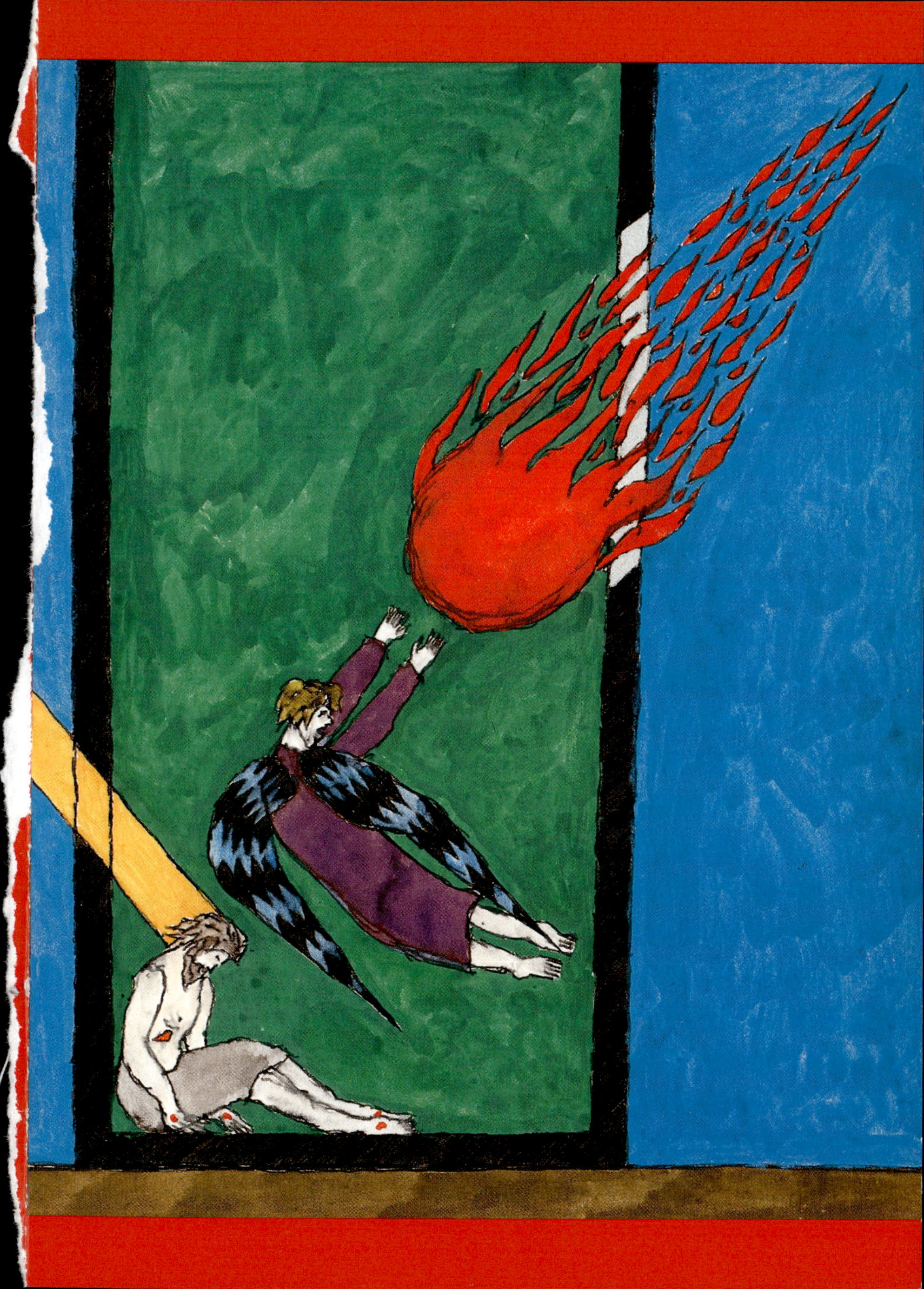

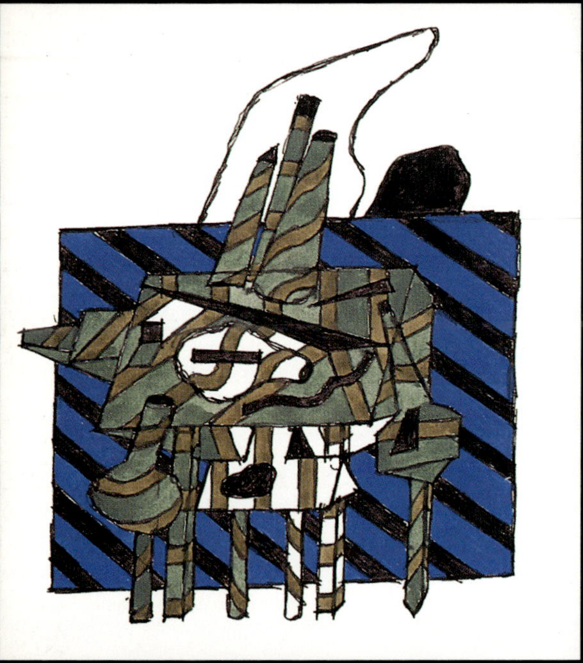

Andalusian Wall Houses, *1995*

1 2 3 4 5 6 7 9 10 11 12 13 14 15 16 17 18 19 20 21 22 23 24 25 26 27 28 29 30 31 32

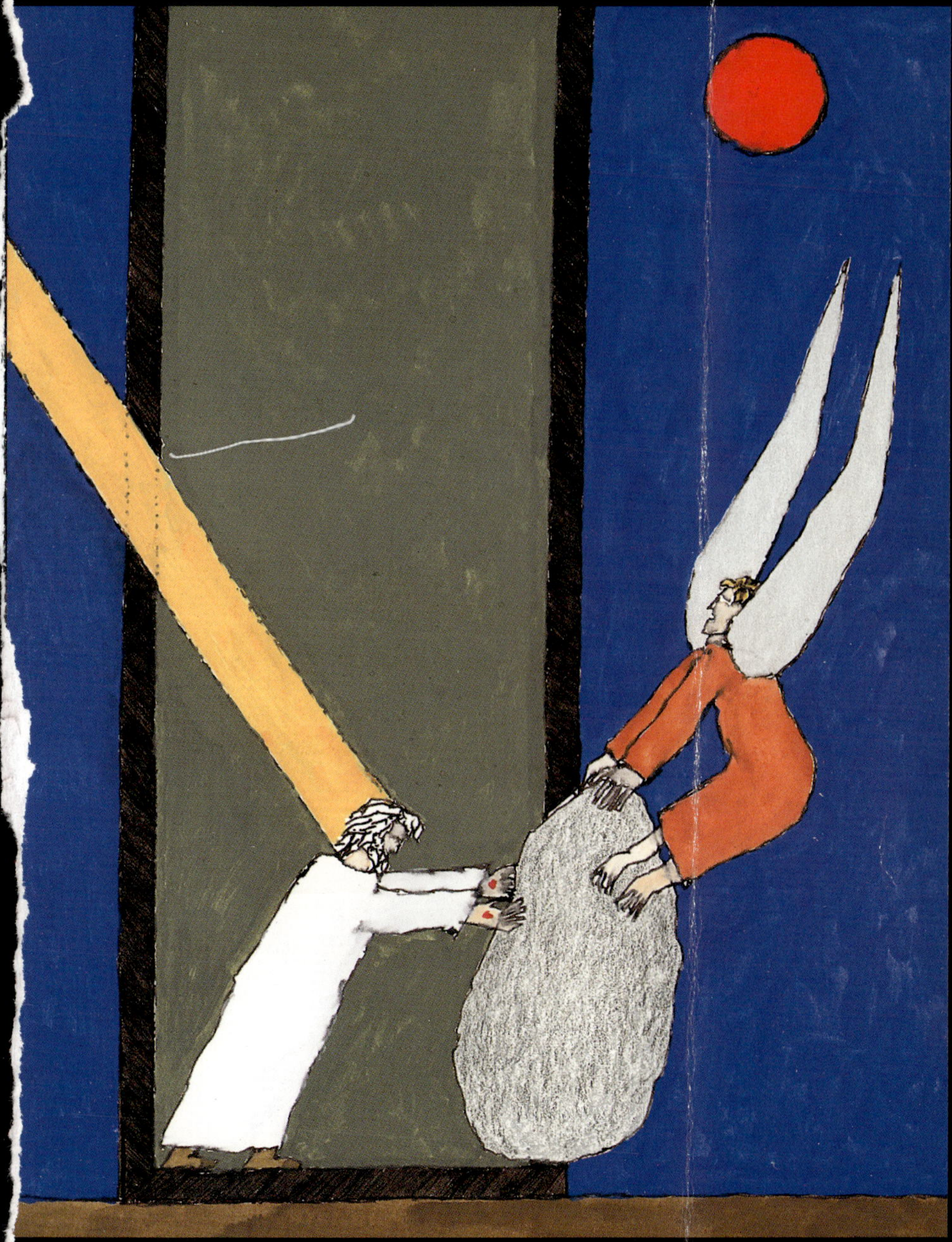

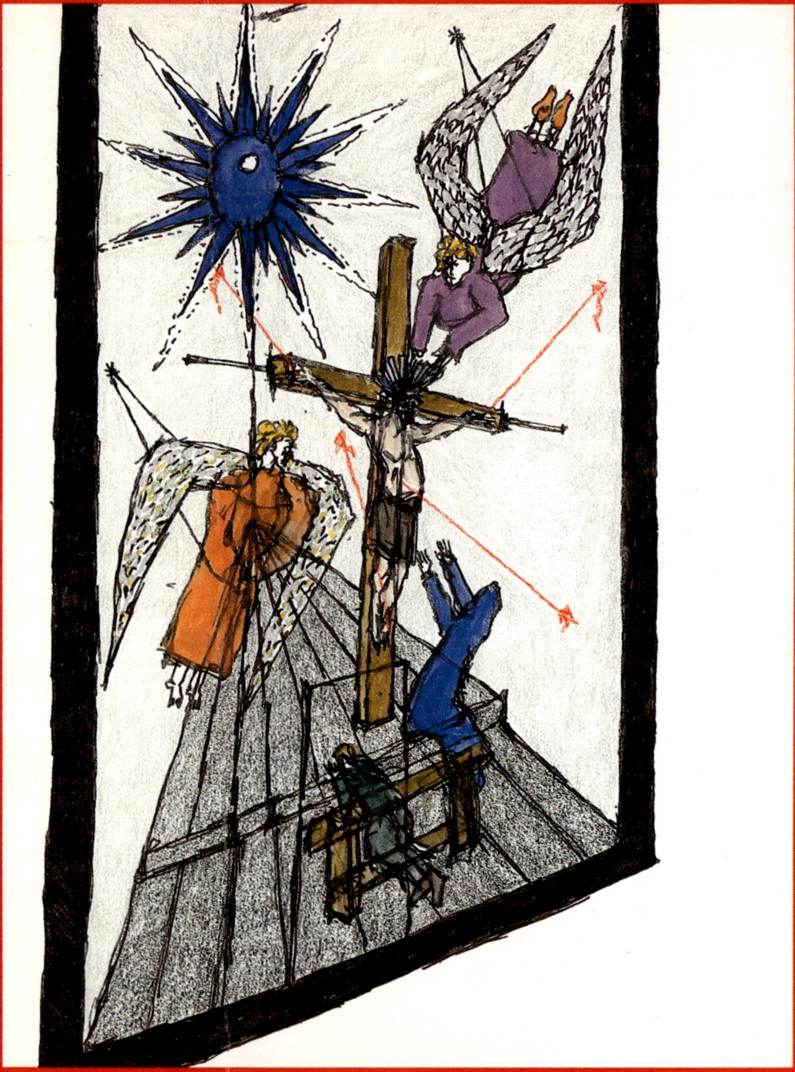

Sanctuary 1, *1999–2000*

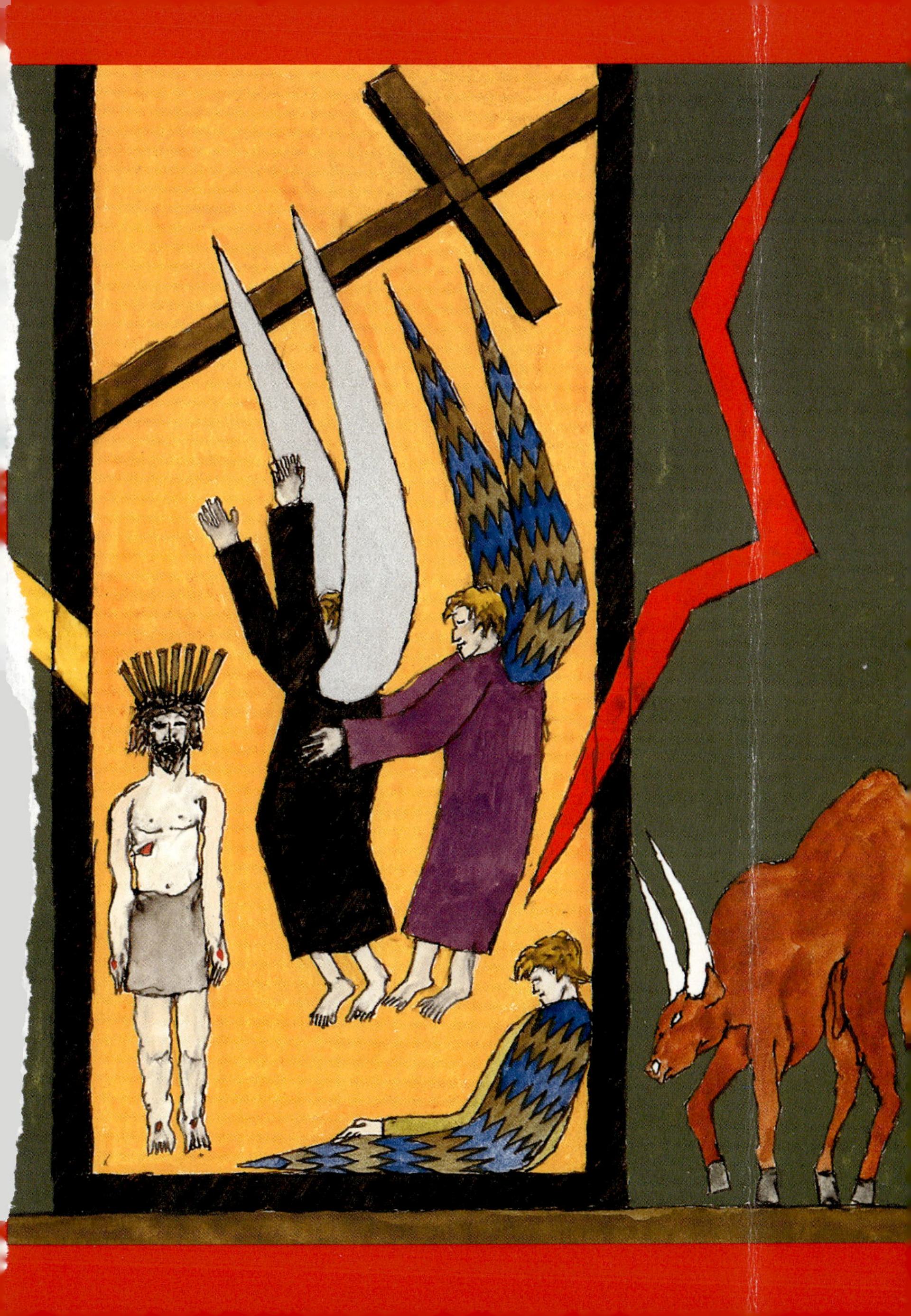

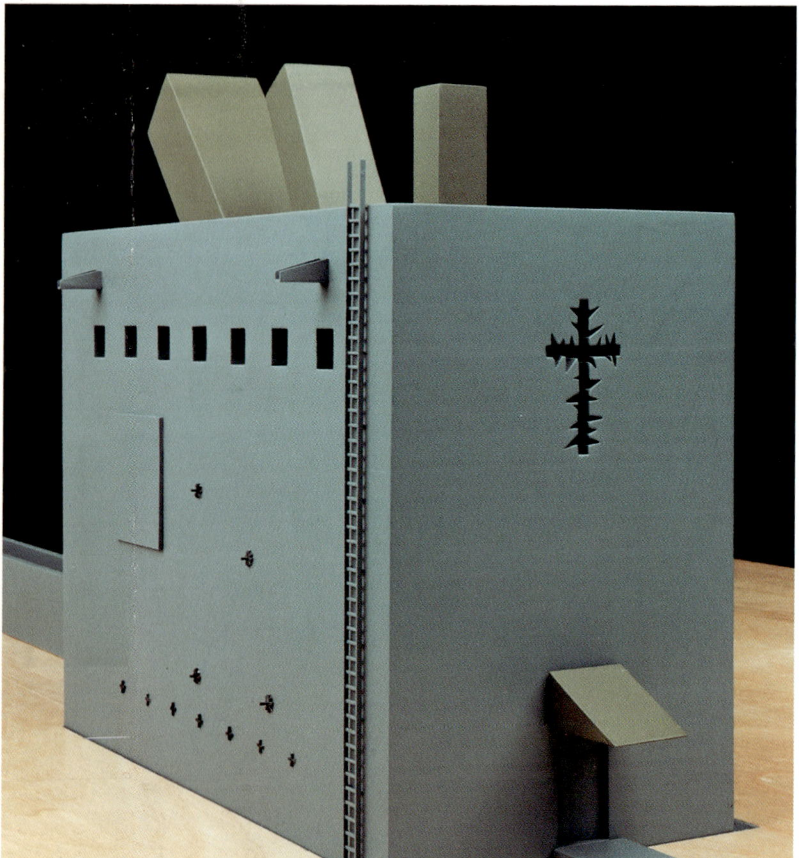

Christ Chapel, *1996* (detail)

1 2 3 4 5 6 7 8 9 ■ 11 12 13 14 15 16 17 18 19 20 21 22 23 24 25 26 27 28 29 30 31 32

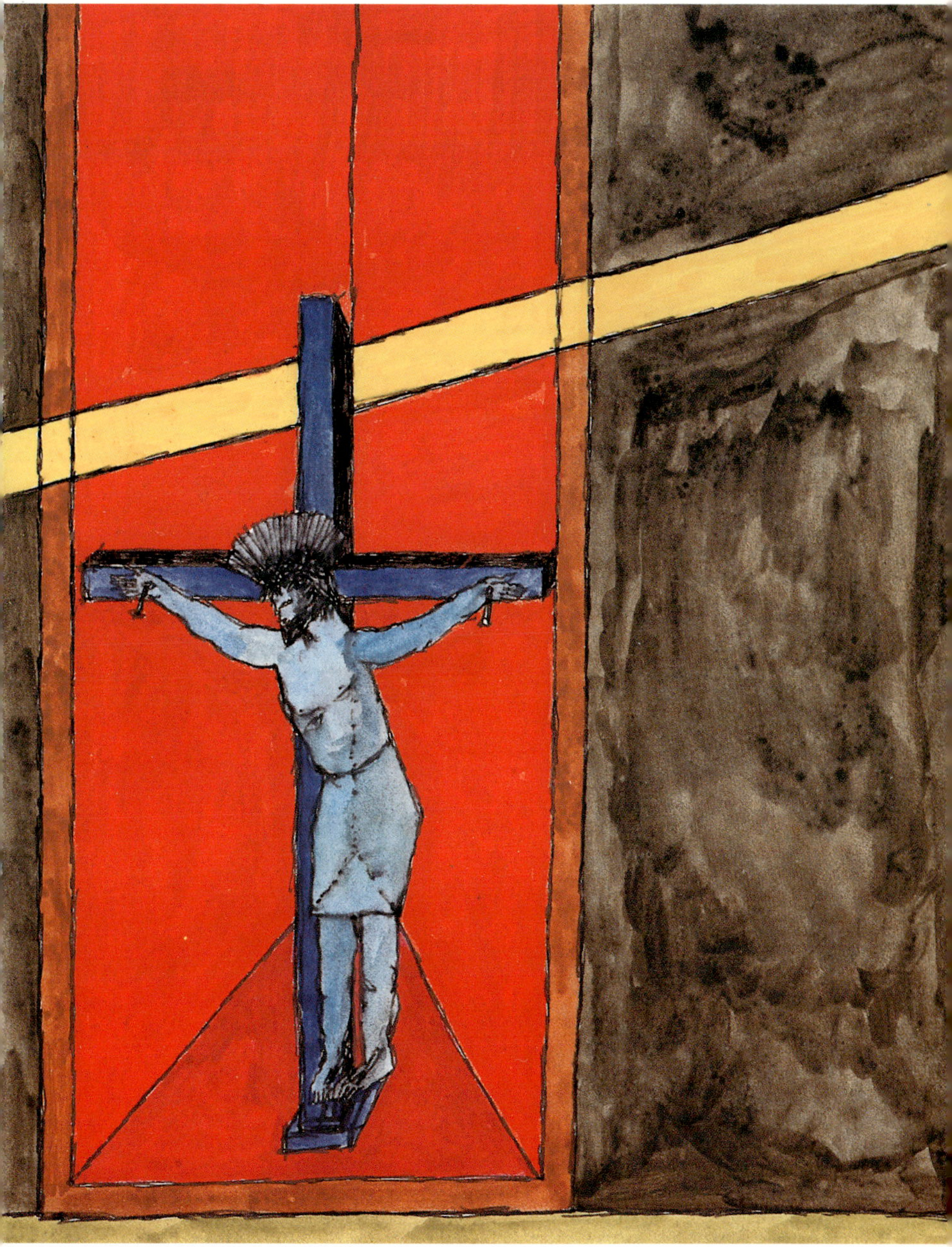

1
2
3
4
5
6
7
8
9
10
■
12
13
14
15
16
17
18
19
20
21
22
23
24
25
26
27
28
29
30
31
32

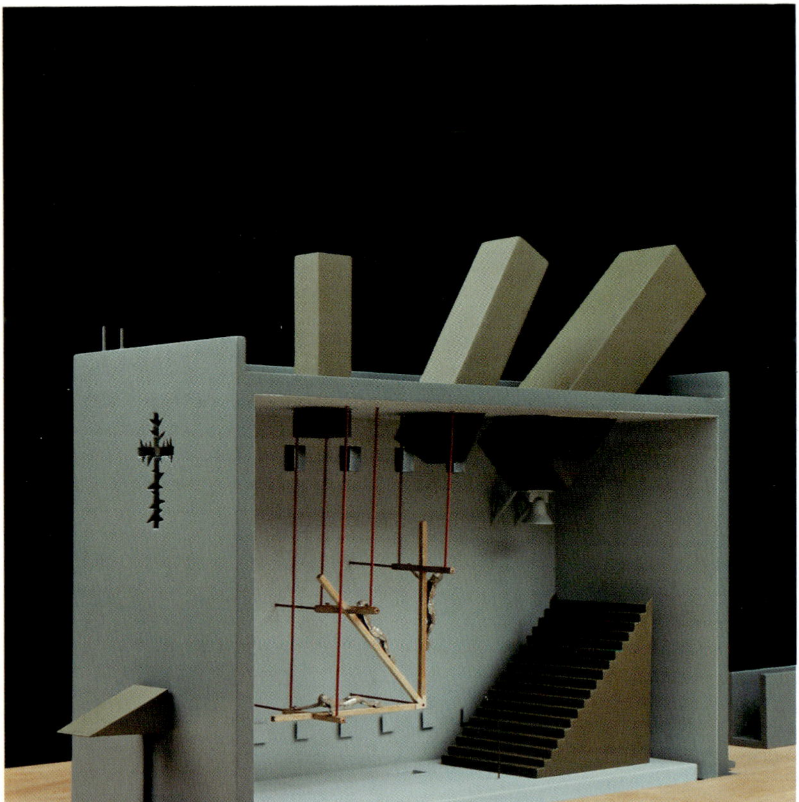

Christ Chapel, *1996* (detail)

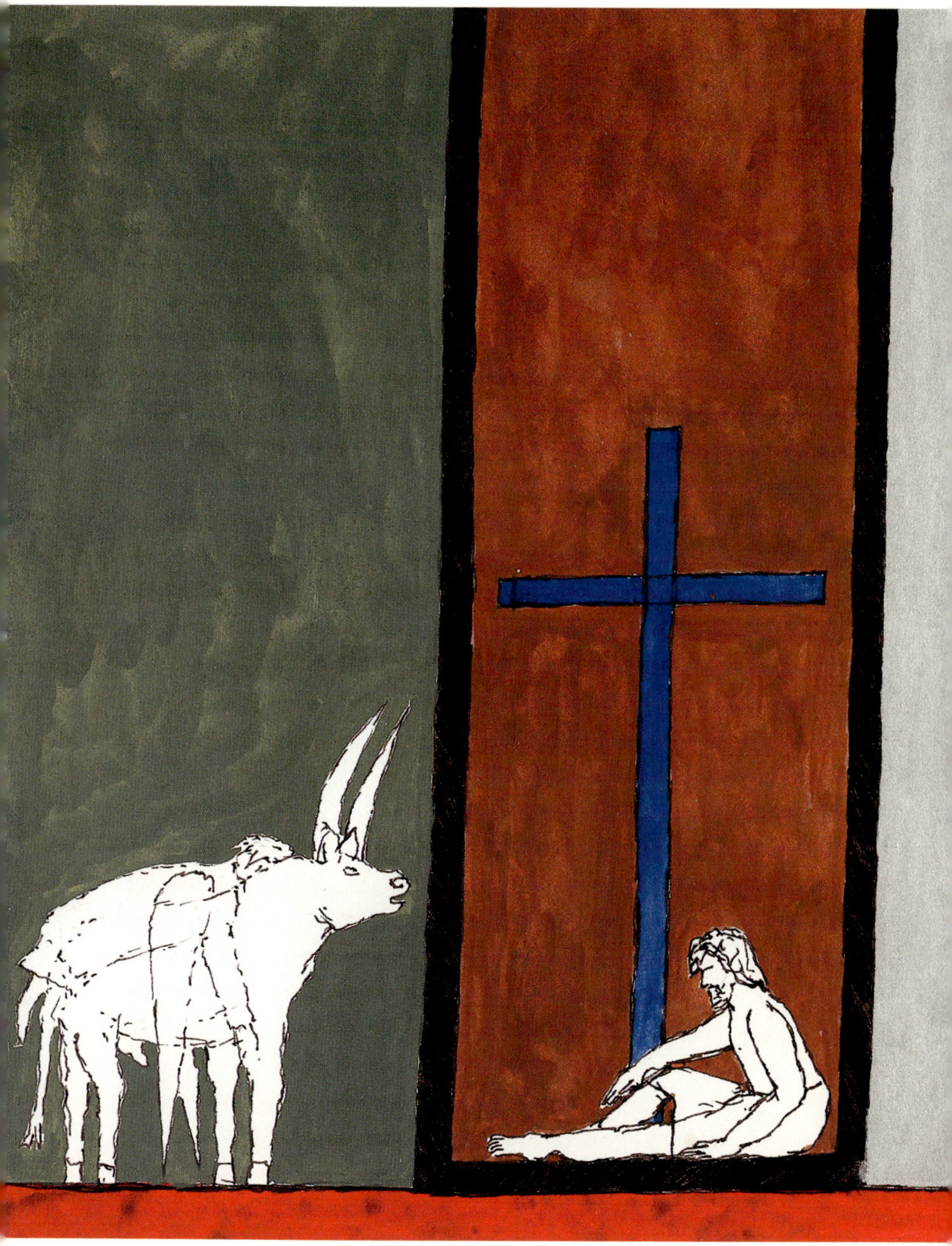

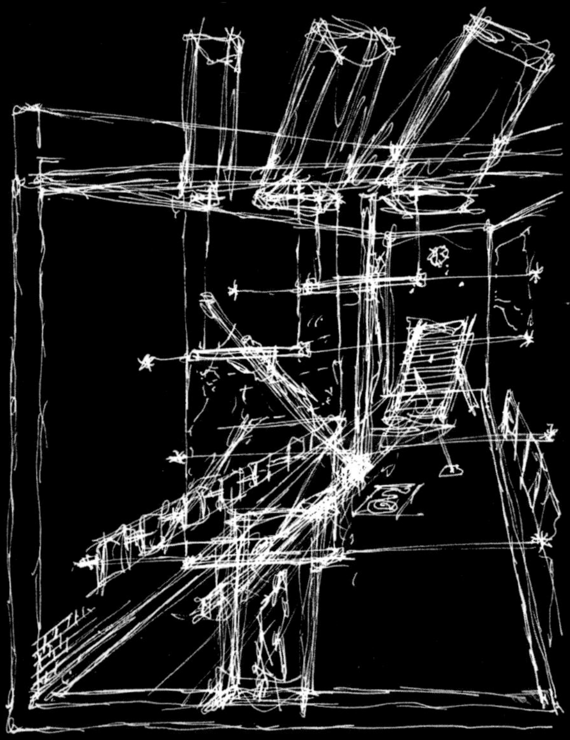

Interior Perspective for Christ Chapel, *1996* (negative image)

1
2
3
4
5
6
7
8
9
10
11
■
13
14
15
16
17
18
19
20
21
22
23
24
25
26
27
28
29
30
31
32

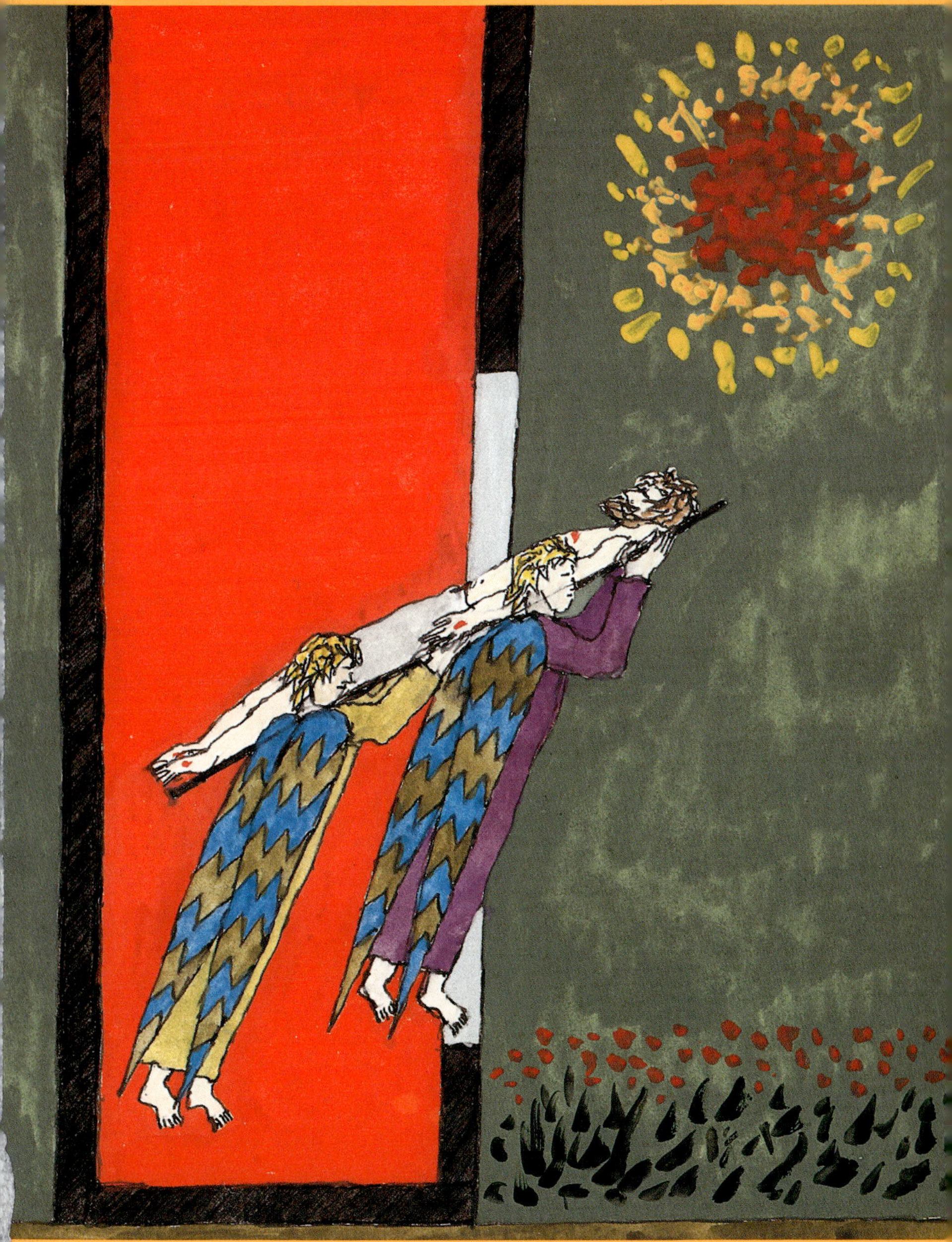

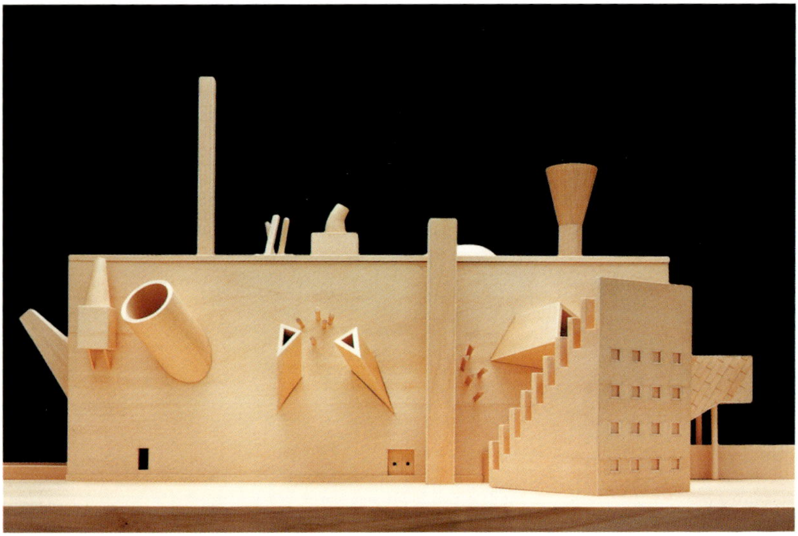

Cathedral, *1996*

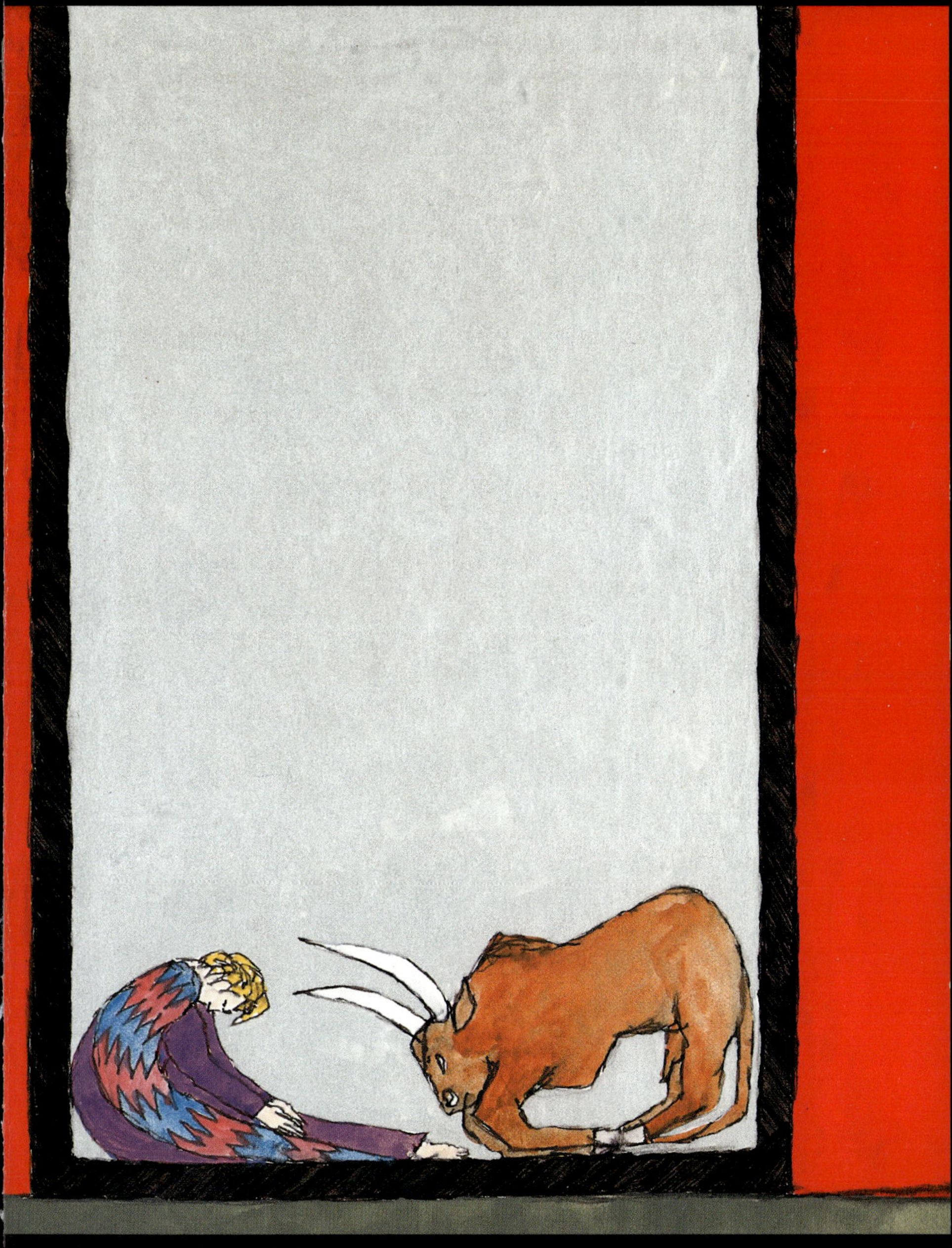

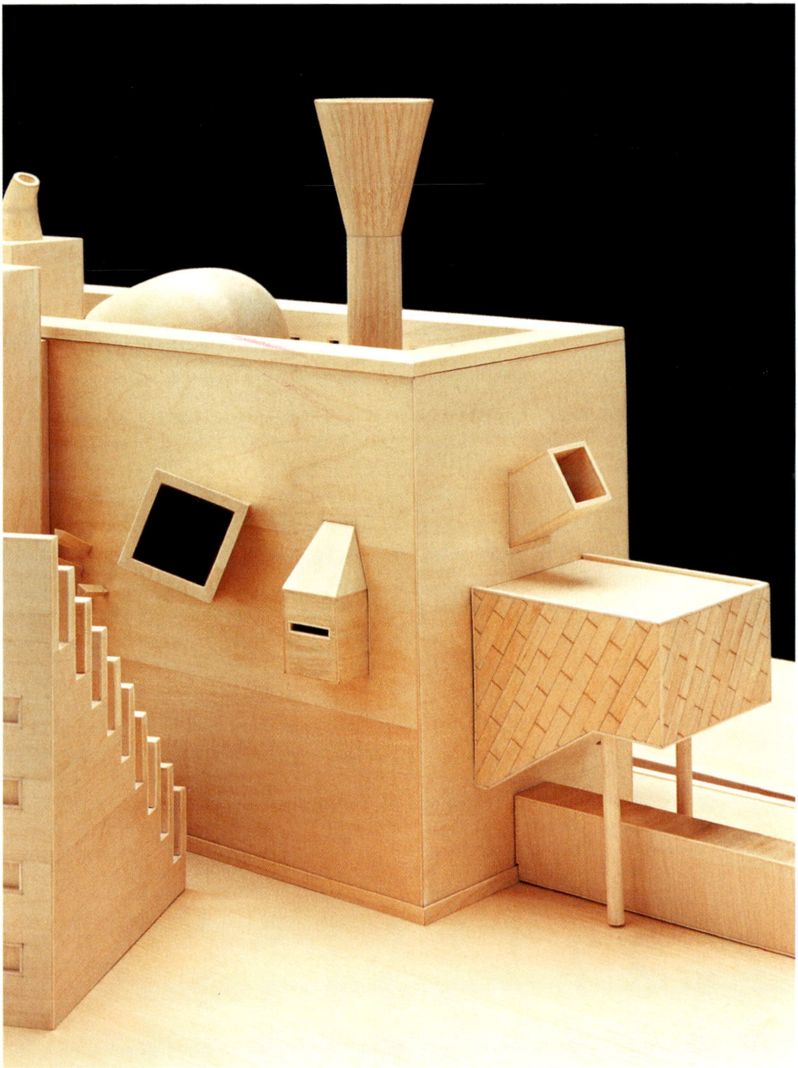

1
2
3
4
5
6
7
8
9
10
11
12
13
14
15
16
17
18
19
■
21
22
23
24
25
26
27
28
29
30
31
32

Cathedral, *1996* (detail)

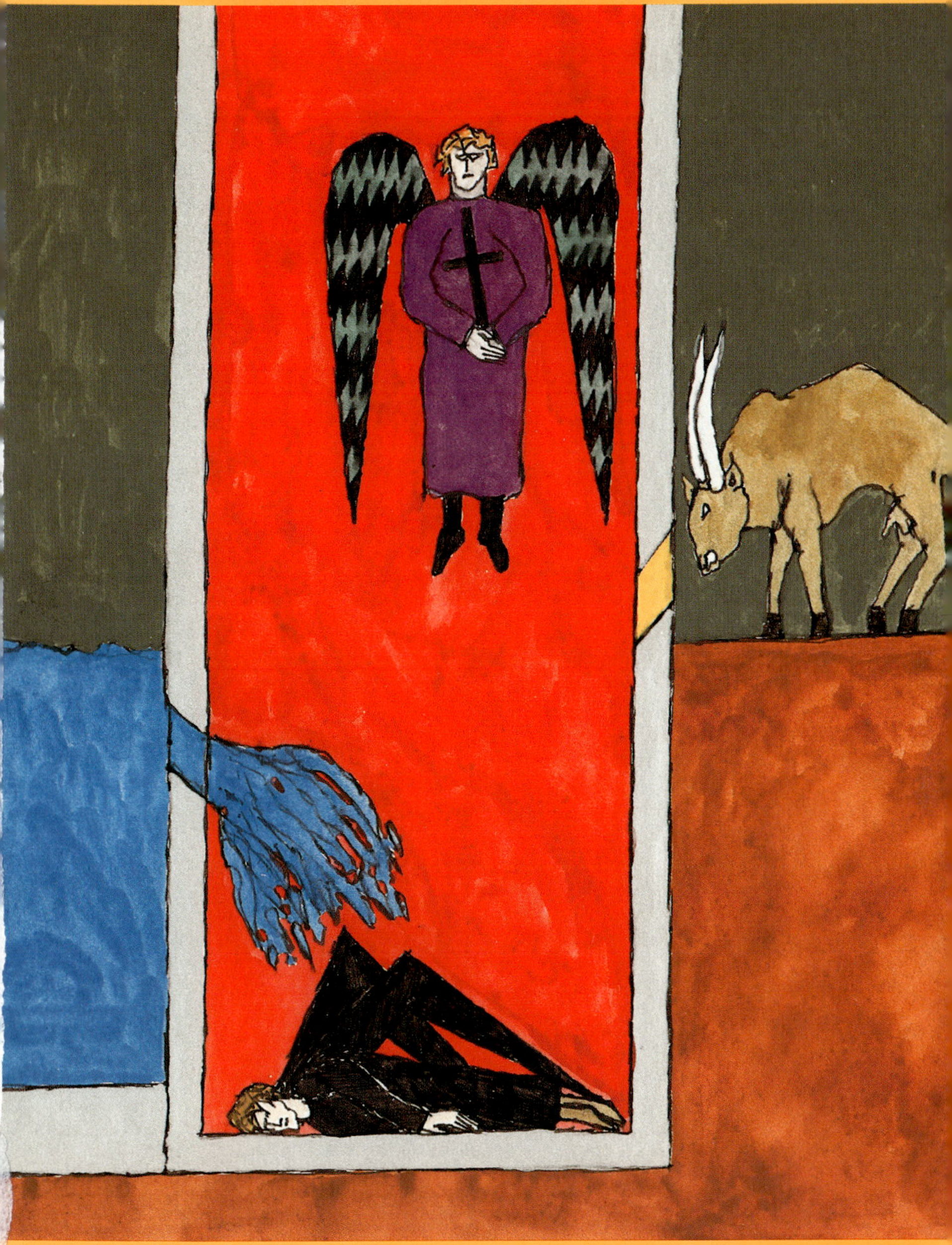

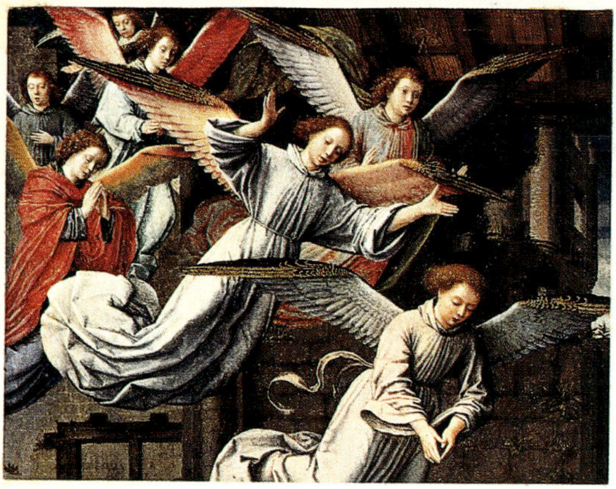

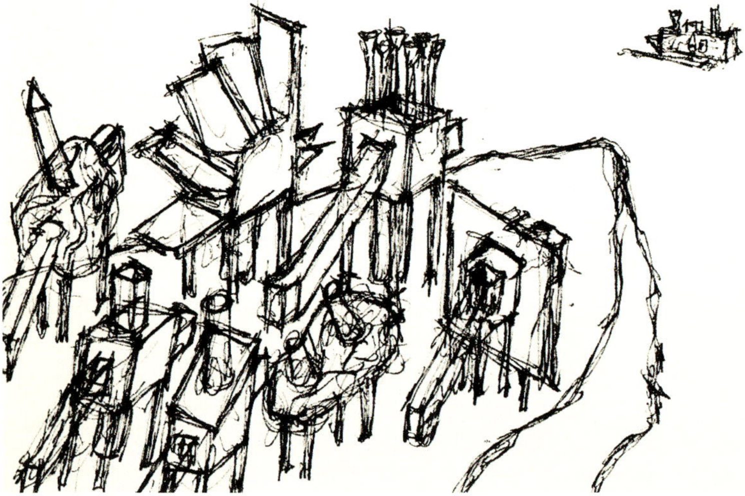

Bird's-Eye View of Structures Overlooking Cathedral Site and
a Postcard Painting of the Annunciation, *1996*

1
2
3
4
5
6
7
8
9
10
11
12
13
14
15
16
17
18
19
20
■
22
23
24
25
26
27
28
29
30
31
32

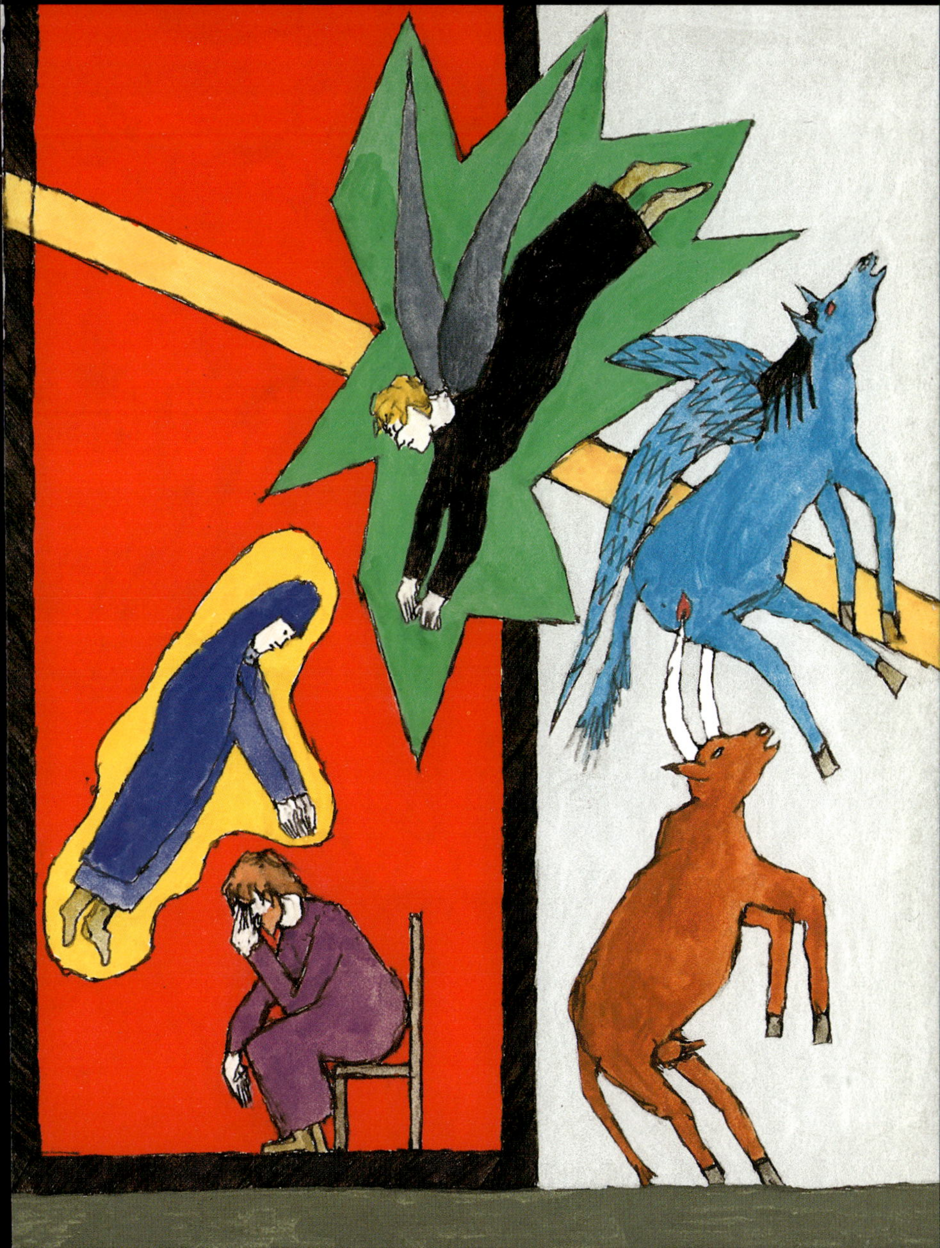

1
2
3
4
5
6
7
8
9
10
11
12
13
14
15
16
17
18
19
20
21
22
23
24
25
26
27
■
29
30
31
32

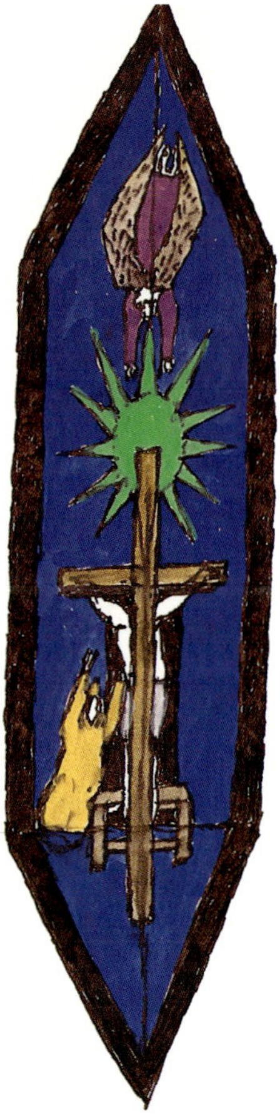

Sanctuary 1, *1999–2000*

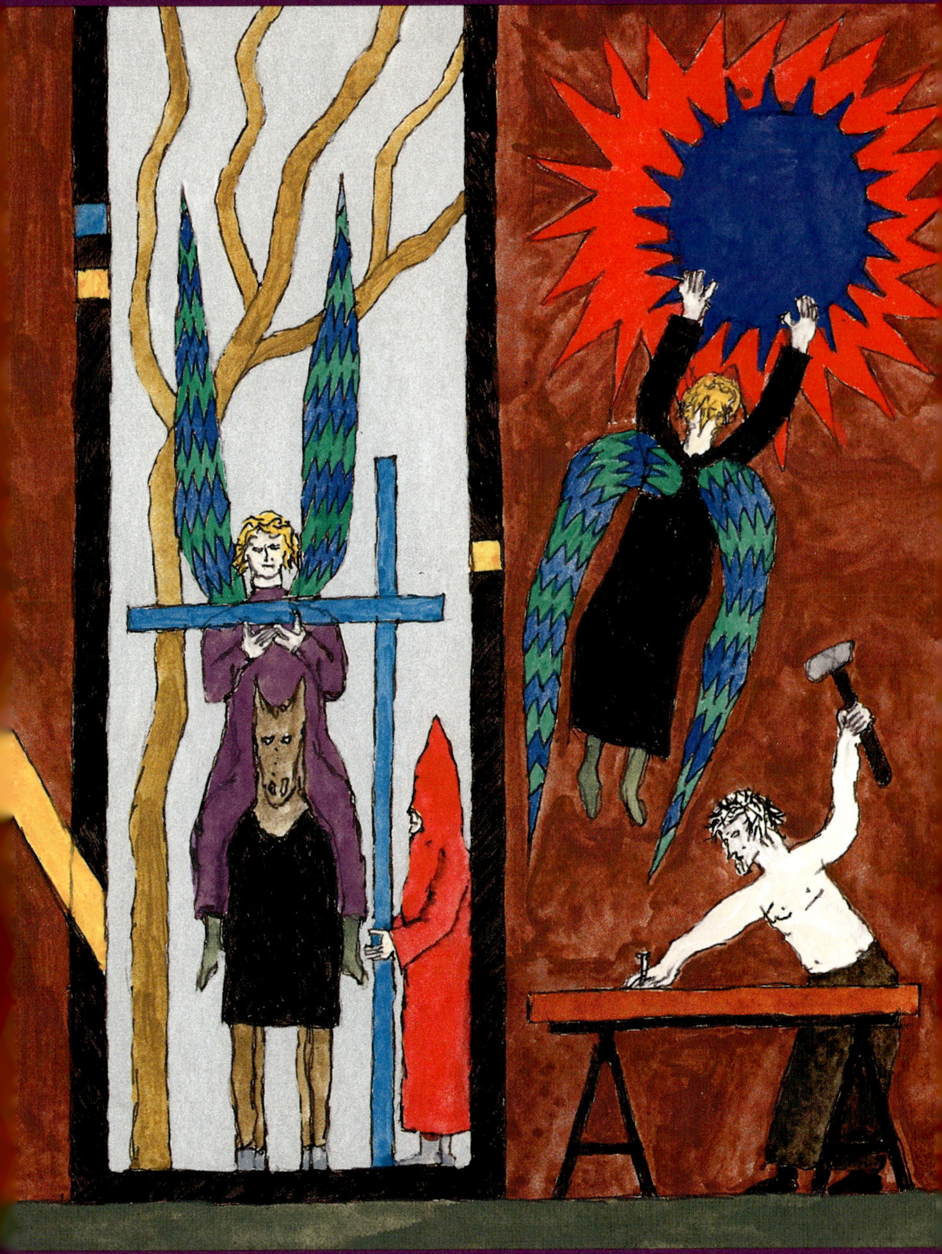

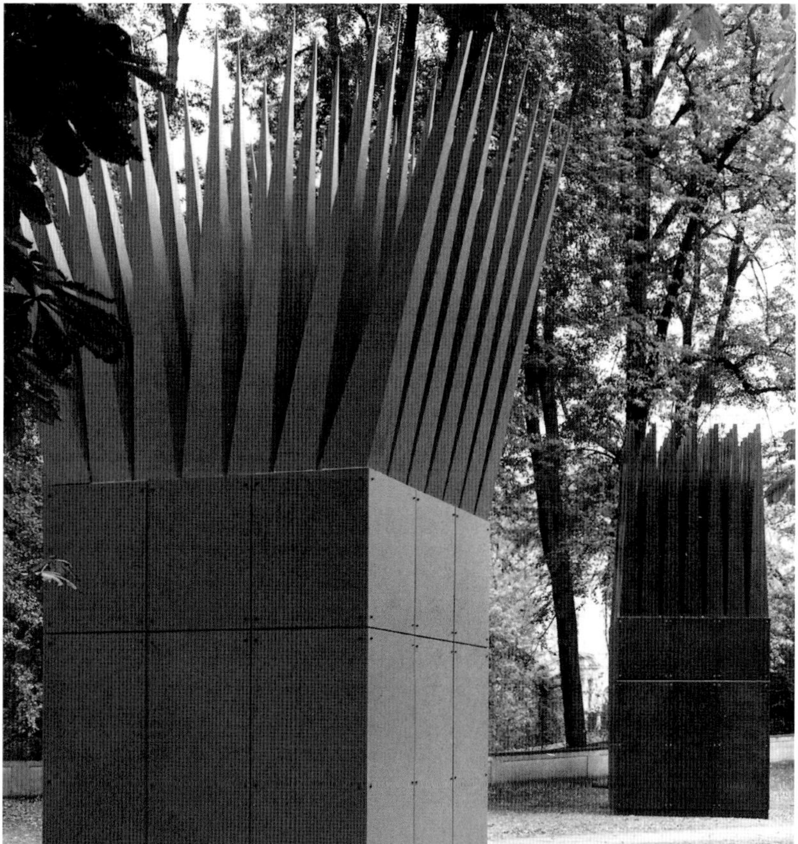

1 2 3 4 5 6 7 8 9 10 11 12 13 14 15 16 17 18 19 20 21 22 23 24 25 26 27 28 ■ 30 31 32

House of the Suicide *and* House of the Mother of the Suicide, *1991*

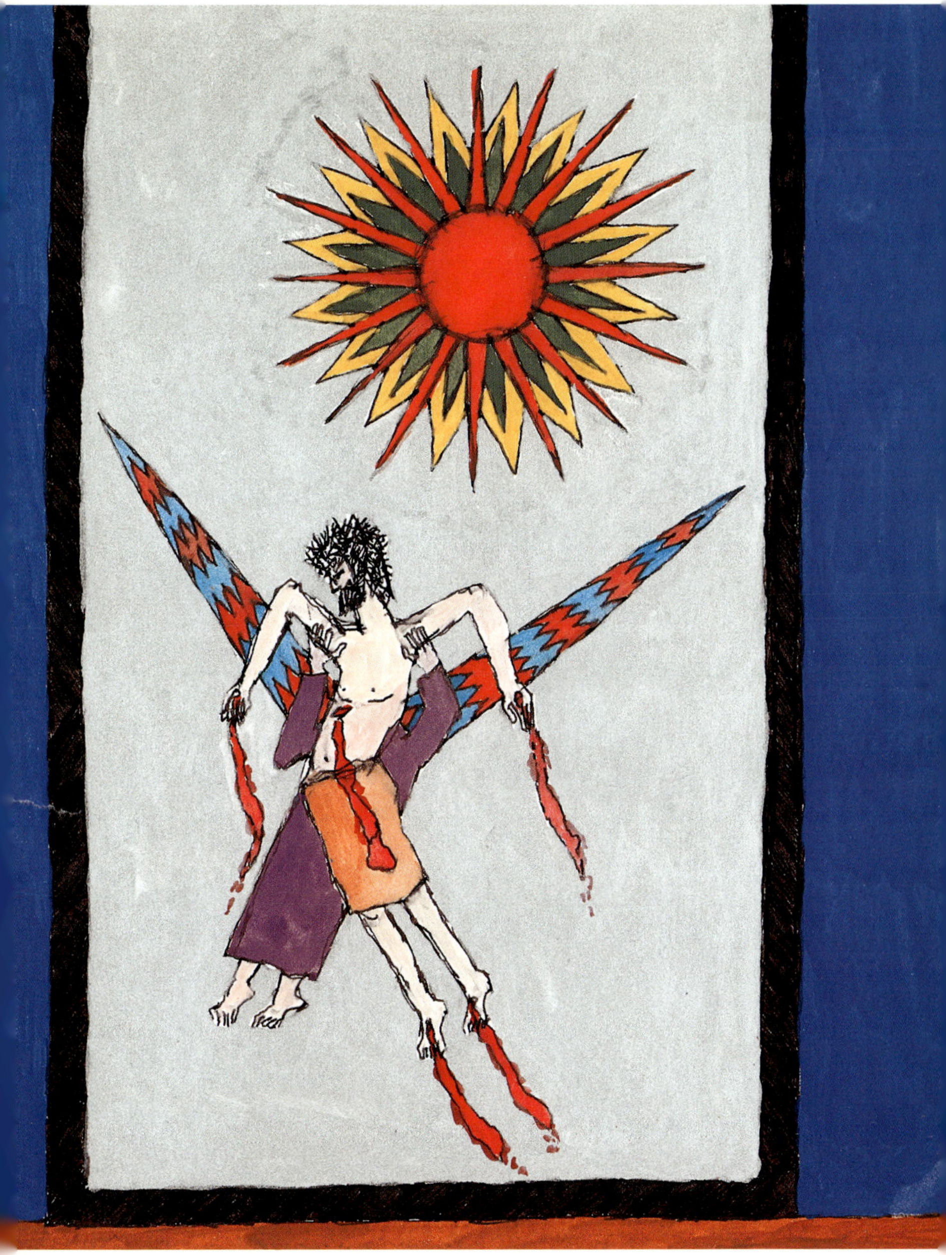

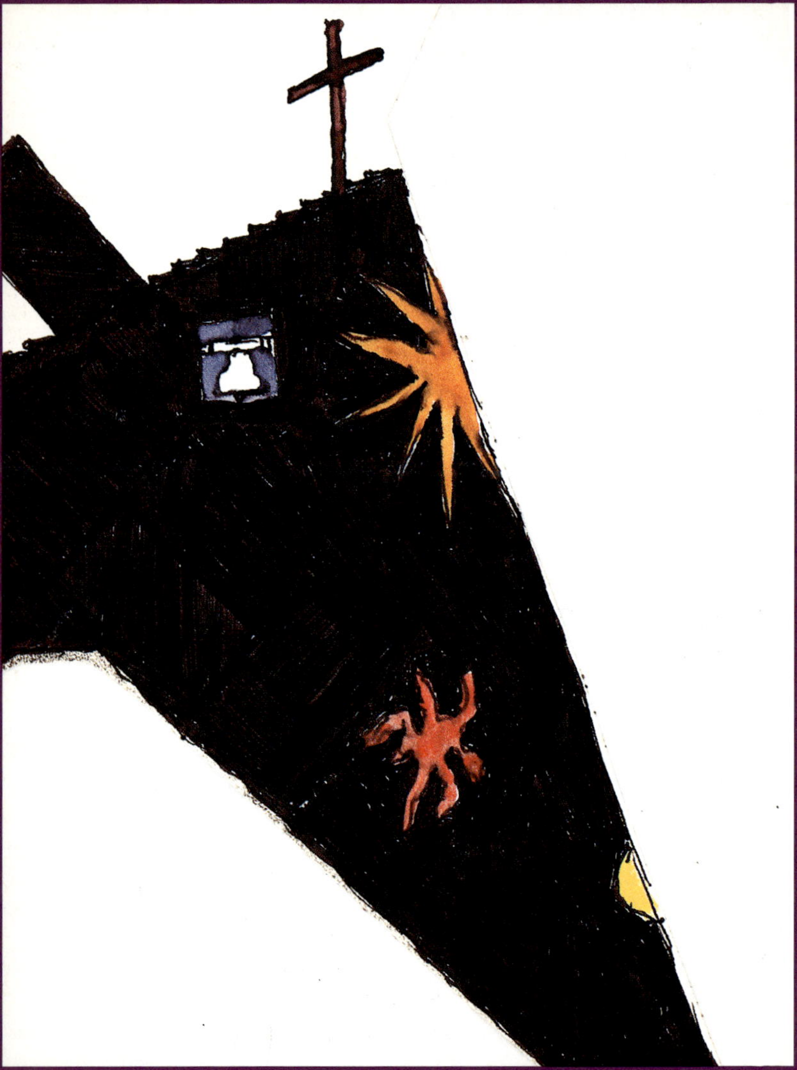

Sanctuary 3, *1999–2000* (detail)

1 2 3 4 5 6 7 8 9 10 11 12 13 14 15 16 17 18 19 20 21 22 23 24 25 26 27 28 29 ■ 31 32

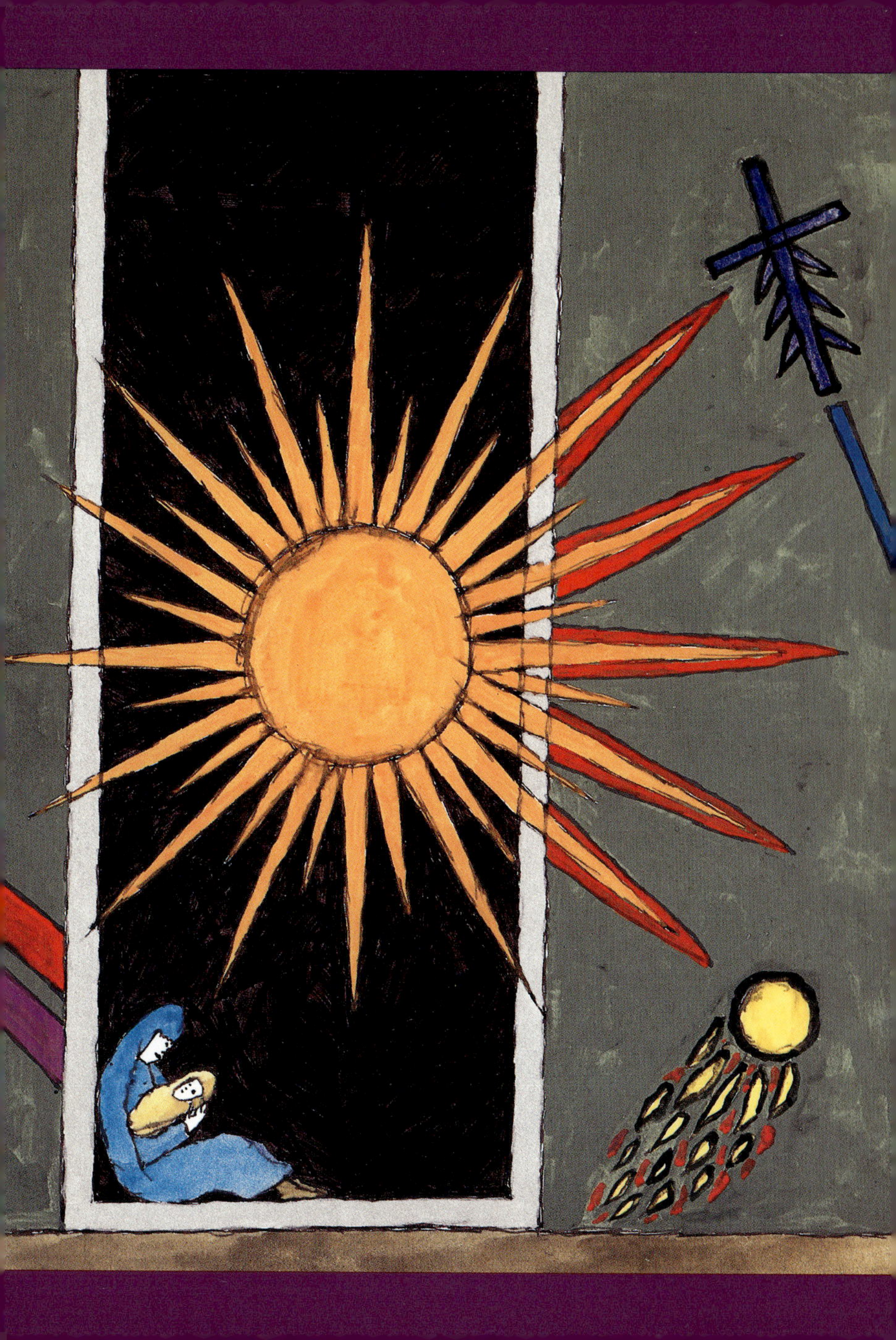

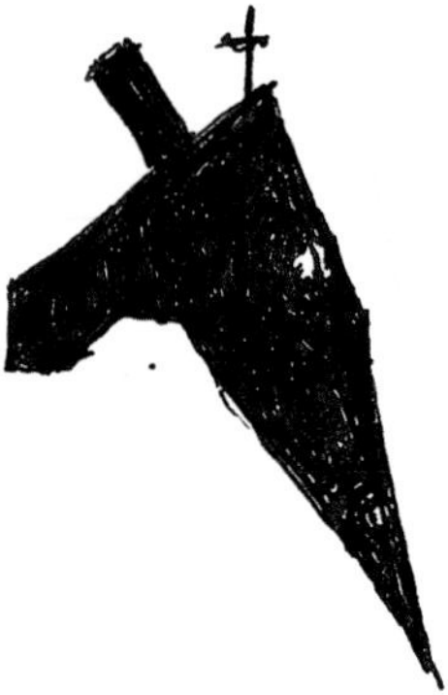

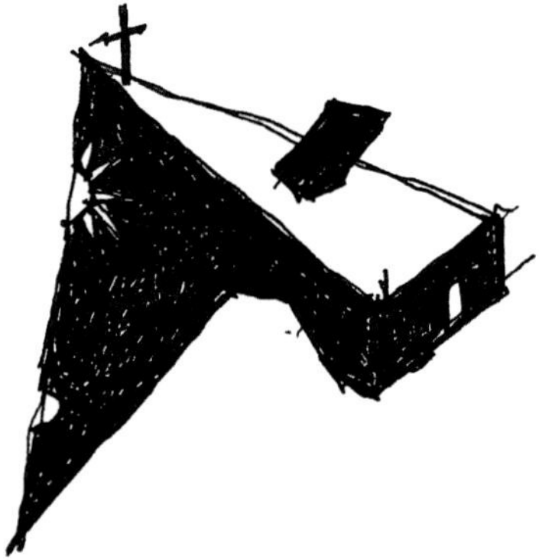

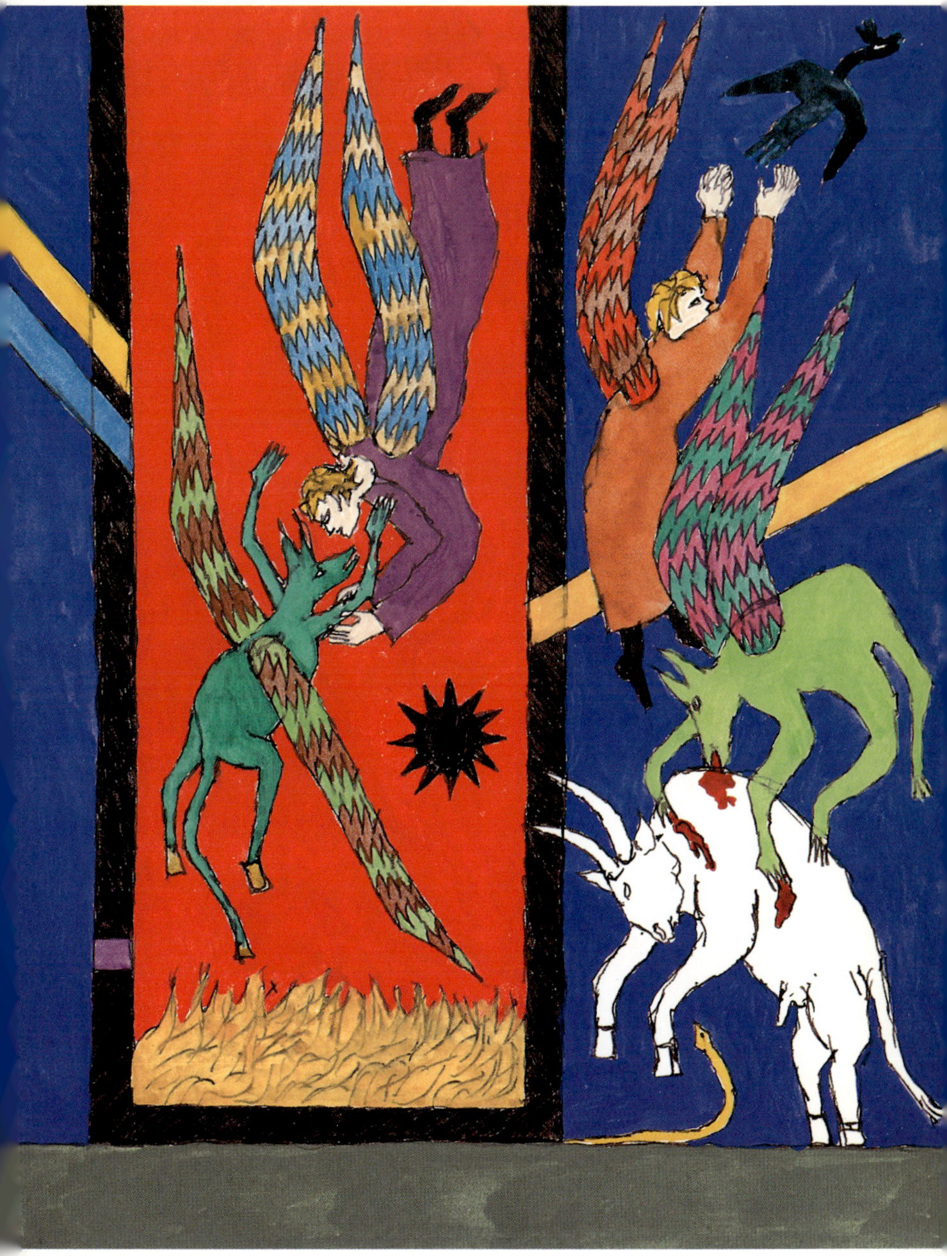

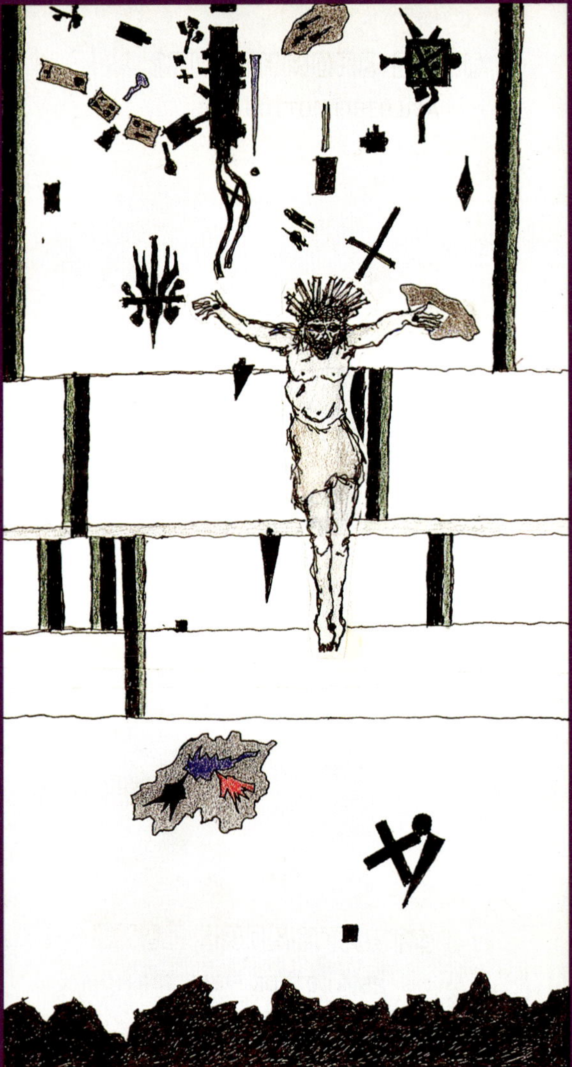

1
2
3
4
5
6
7
8
9
10
11
12
13
14
15
16
17
18
19
20
21
22
23
24
25
26
27
28
29
30
31

Sanctuary 3, *1999–2000* (detail)

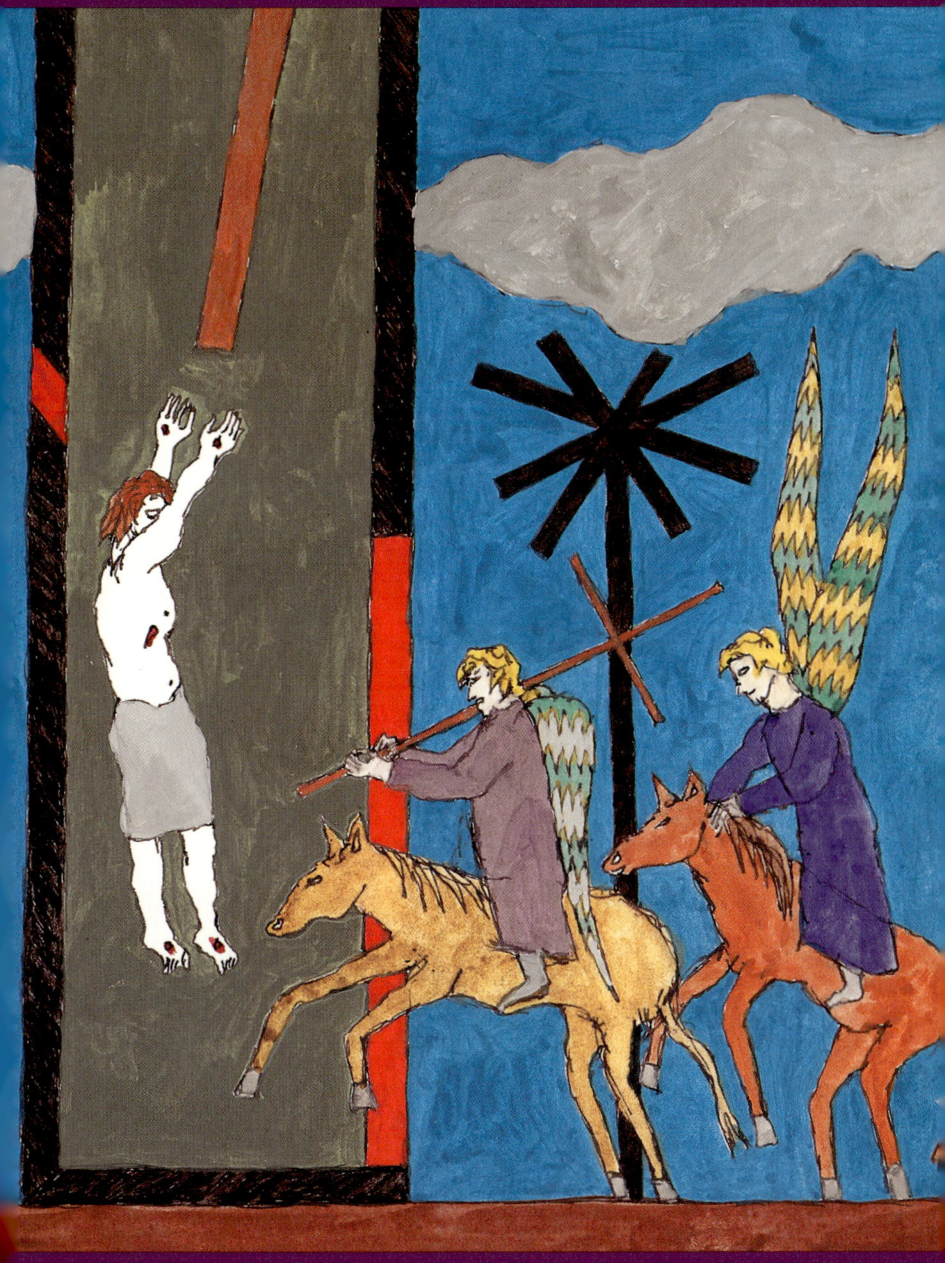

ARCHITECTURE'S DESTINY

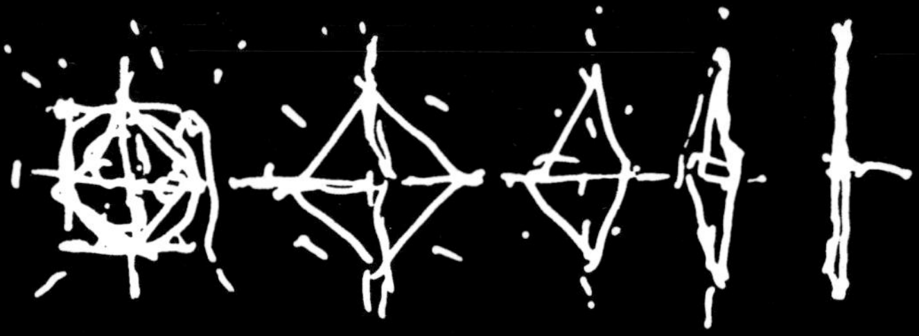

K. Michael Hays

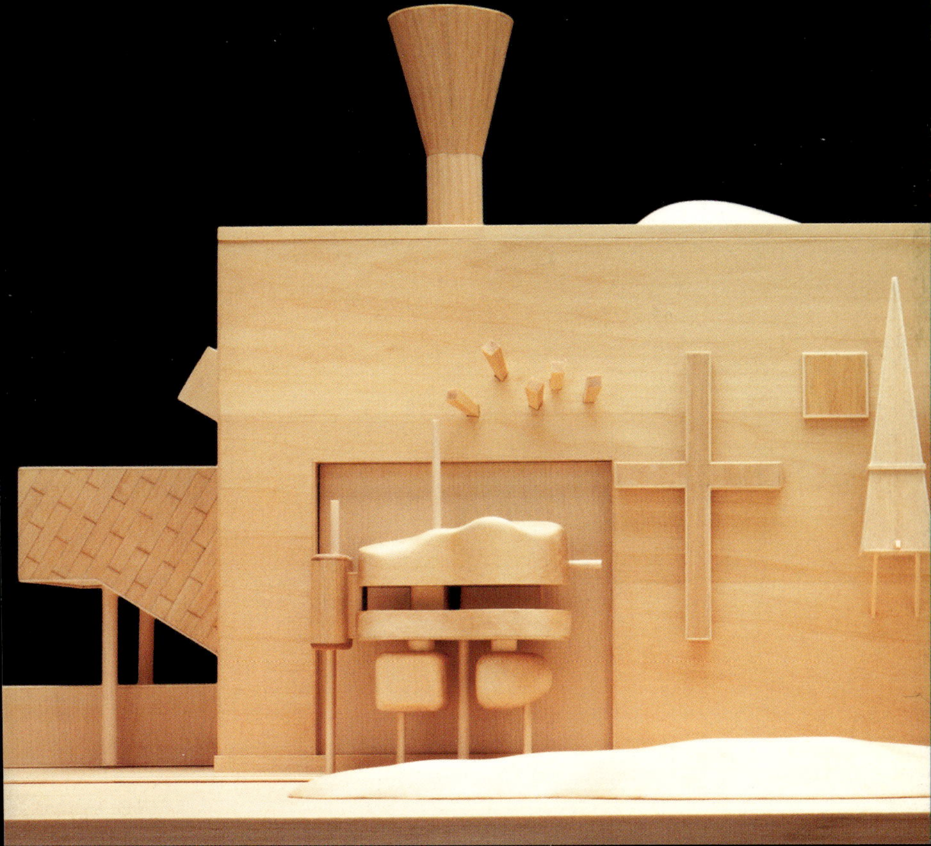

Historians of architecture will correctly concentrate the significance of John Hejduk's work at his "discovery" of the first Wall House around 1969 (it seemed as if it had always been there in the architecture unconscious) and his reinvention (after the Italian *maschera*, after Inigo Jones) of the architectural masque, which began in 1981 with *Berlin Masque*, though *Cemetery for the Ashes of Thought* (1974) already anticipated it. The importance of these two moments in Hejduk's career is undoubted. But the destiny of these works, the horizon toward which both the Wall Houses and the Masques are pulled, stretches just behind a different set of projects completed between 1998 and 2000, gathered together here under the rubric "Sanctuaries." They include, among others, *Christ Chapel* and *Cathedral*—represented here in models commissioned by the Canadian Centre for Architecture—and the suite of thirty-two drawings in The Menil Collection entitled *Enclosures*.[1]

The full argument for the claim that the fulfillment of Hejduk's architecture lies in these last works would require a more extensive analysis of the multiple, idiosyncratic codings of his architectural elements than is possible in this volume—his menagerie of angels, animals, martyrs, and machines; his stylistic preference for basic geometric forms and elemental biomorphism (buildings that seem to have hair, beaks, eyes, and legs) combined with typological variations on theaters, periscopes, funnels, traps, chapels, and labyrinths; his thematic explorations of falls from grace, itinerancy, passage, and transformation; and above all, his belief in architecture as sanctuary—sanctuary for art, for culture, for the enduring rituals that mark us as human, for the human spirit itself. In the long run, however, the content of Hejduk's architecture will always stand judged by its form, whose deep structural development is the most certain index to the many semantic, allegorical, and experiential possibilities that it constructs. So it is to form and its perception that we must first turn.

In an early (1963) but often repeated explication of the Diamond Houses (a series of carefully calibrated and measured formal transformations that owe much to Mondrian, Le Corbusier, and Mies van der Rohe), Hejduk constructs a diagram of the history of architectural space, declaring the paradigmatic space of the present to be the compression on a vertical two-dimensional surface of the space generated by the two legs of a right angle. The logic goes something like this: If the primitive condition of architecture is the square, the square is, nevertheless, generated as the isometric projection of a diamond, making the diamond paradoxically prior to, or more primitive than, the square. Yet, if the diamond is understood perceptually as the plan diagram of an architectural space rather than as a two-dimensional graphic shape, then the most fundamental percept of the space of the diamond is another square, one that results from collapsing the two legs of the diamond's right angle, now projected as vertical planes or walls, onto a picture plane. In other words, the diamond returns to the square when it is perceived in perspective. This is true whether the viewer is outside the diamond plan—the protruding exterior corner reduced to an invisible line on the perceptual plane—or inside the plan, the corner now retreating, but with no perceivable difference between the two perspectives.

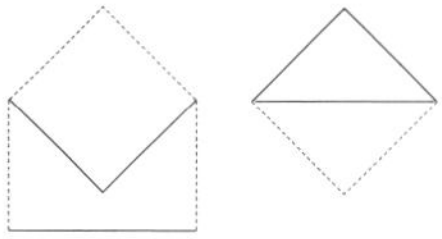

What is more, this compression of deep space onto a flat elevational surface is homologous with both the picture plane onto which the perspectival space of the Renaissance is projected

(Alberti's famous slice through the "cone" of vision) and the anti-Albertian canvas of the Cubist still life (think of the table of the still life tilted up vertically), in which perspective's beginning and end, the vanishing point, is always absent. Developing the classicist-modernist axioms of flatness versus depth and opacity versus transparency, Hejduk understands this percept—the image of the flattening or collapsing of deep space onto the square vertical plane—as at once the most basic element of any architecture, the summation of the history of architectural space to date, and a historically specific phenomenon. For the percept itself is located on the crease in time between the past and the future. "It's a beautiful distance," he declares of the space and time seen backward and forward from this plane. "As you go back into space it gets into deeper perspective, it gets less clear and you can never really complete it, because that's the unknown, it isn't fixed. So it gets darker. As you get closer to the present, it's clearer. On the plane of the present is that horizontal armature, which is the hypotenuse; you just speculate on futures." (*Mask of Medusa*, 50) The diagram included in the title of my essay is Hejduk's shorthand notation for the story of this spatial apparatus. It is for him the fundamental mechanism by which architecture pushes its most basic logic, its genetic code, out into the realm of the visible. And that story—

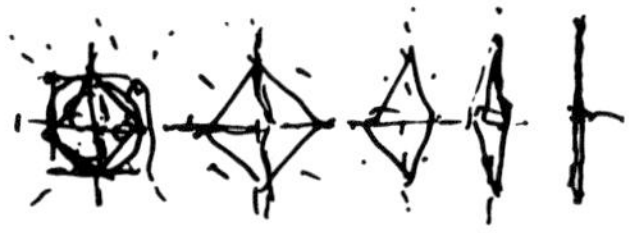

the theme of deep space collapsed onto a vertical surface—subtends the entire trajectory of Hejduk's career. Its last intersection is at *Enclosures*, which form the core of this book.

The research of the Diamond House and its perceptual screen made possible the discovery of the Wall House, Hejduk's architectural still life of biomorphic forms and fragments of objects now hovering in elevation in front of a thin, taut wall plane, rather than deployed back, deep in plan, as in the Diamond Houses. "The wall represents the same condition as the 'moment of the hypotenuse' in the Diamond Houses—it's the moment of greatest repose, and at the same time the greatest tension. It is a moment of passage. The wall heightens that sense of passage, and by the same token, its thinness heightens the sense of it being just a momentary condition ...what I call the moment of the 'present.'" (67) One thinks of Picasso's still life, *The Architect's Table,* and its attempt to make a new pictorial order out of perception itself through the conventions and the procedures of painting. The Wall House is the architect's version of the Cubist dream of a new order, with all its contradictions, with all its totalizing tendencies, and with all its world-making ambitions.

At the same time, the Wall House makes explicit a condition that was only implied in the Diamond Houses but will be explored in subsequent projects: The viewing subject of architecture is not just the observer of an object focused as an image and arrayed before him or her on the plane of perception. Rather, the subject is also produced by the architecture, for the architecture—or better, Architecture, in a generalized, disciplinary sense—exerts a defining force back on the subject, and in the same vertical plane, so to speak. As I have said, Hejduk understands the elevational surface, together with its temporal dimension, as the topos of the cultural reserve of spatial organizations, of which each moment of architectural experience is just one instance. All of architecture's latent possibilities, the entire architectural language, lies waiting just behind the plane.

"It's physical by memory," he says of this plane at one point. (50) His elevational surface—the Wall as a signifying apparatus—contains the sedimented conventions of the discipline, the codes of architecture built up over centuries from Alberti to Le Corbusier and Mies, overlain with qualifications and values, shot through with the ideals and ideologies of past generations. It is "all-encompassing," (62) "it's an expanding universe. It's emanating from a center; it's an explosive center." (50) And you are not just looking at it, "you are in it," Hejduk says. "You become an element of an internal system of organisms." (62) The wall is auratic and replete; it pushes back at the looker. As Walter Benjamin noted, "To perceive the aura of an object we look at means to invest it with the ability to look at us in return. This experience corresponds to the data of the *mémoire involontaire*."[2]

But Hejduk's Wall focuses that involuntary memory, the vaporous recollection of architecture's own history, in the present instance of embodied vision. Its corporeal-temporal dimension keeps what might otherwise freeze into a final reified image from ever fixing itself. Its mnemonics are emergent rather than residual, and any memories produced must be constantly negotiated. Indeed, in this respect, Hejduk's own comments on the Wall apparatus are akin to the famous contemporaneous story (1964) by the French psychoanalytic theorist Jacques Lacan. Lacan writes of seeing a sardine can floating on the sea, glittering in the sun, and looking, it seems, back at the young Lacan, situating him, pinning him to a fundamental lack in his own self and to his own decentered moment. The experience led Lacan to his theory of the double articulation of the subject as both viewer of the object and under the regard of the object, pictured by what Lacan calls its "gaze." Lacan diagrams this in a way very similar to Hejduk's spatial apparatus. On the one hand, there is the perspectival cone of the Renaissance, the *trompe l'oeil* that produces and organizes the image for us on the

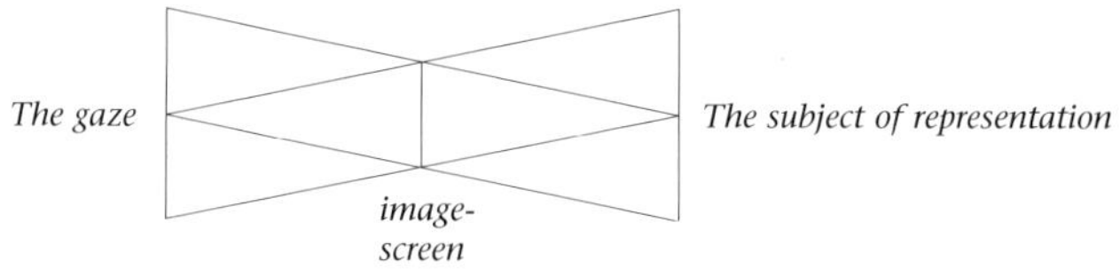

transparent picture plane. On the other hand is an opposite cone that emanates from the object itself, like a projected light coming at us (like the light from the sardine can), which we cannot control. In this projected light, coinciding with the plane of the image, is an interrupting screen, opaque rather than transparent. Lacan calls this the *dompte regard,* a membrane or blotter that subdues or mediates the gaze for us, helping us to negotiate its blinding light. The coincidence of the two planes Lacan calls the "image-screen" or the "mask," and it is this that both determines what can and cannot be seen and how it is seen, and helps us to manage what is seen by giving us a symbolic system with which to represent objects to ourselves and ourselves to others. "Man, in effect, knows how to play with the mask as that beyond which there is the gaze," Lacan states.[3] Hejduk's image-screen (with its similar dialectic of flatness and depth, opacity and transparency), his Mask of Medusa, is his Wall. For both Hejduk and Lacan, the image-screen is a representational apparatus necessary for our social and cultural existence—a historically generated repertoire of images through which we as social subjects are constructed.

Hejduk's Wall Houses, with their space-time membrane—image-screen, wall-mask, elevational chronotope—initiated not only

Hejduk's return to the positive symbolic and narrative potentials of architecture after the structuralist-formalist prohibition of content (think, for example, of Peter Eisenman's contemporaneous house series), but also his proposition of a radical figuration. Against received formal paradigms that insist on diverse objects of a composition being held together by a unifying datum or ground, the Wall Houses broach the possibility of presenting dissonant, elemental architectural figures without a ground, in the sense that for Hejduk the wall is not ground so much as another figure. Together these two features of the Wall Houses—the temporal, narrative dimension and the radical figuration—form the crux of Hejduk's various Masques. In the tradition of the Italian *maschera* and Inigo Jones, the Masques propose various interacting architectural characters and human inhabitants—architectural troubadours, vagabonds, and itinerants—that travel in caravans from city to city (Berlin, Vladivostok, Lancaster, Hanover), twisting the mundane urbanism of their sites into carnivalesque narratives. In the Masques, the subject-object distinction, already challenged in the Wall Houses, is utterly collapsed; for the inhabitants of Hejduk's chosen cities are deterritorialized into their vocations (the workers, the dwellers, the butter women, the bank-key man), buildings likewise are interchangeable pieces of movable mechanical equipment, and the city itself becomes a smooth space of surrealist ambiance and shifting moods that, like the Wall, registers past events and projects possible future ones.

In the Masques we encounter an architecture overtly anthropomorphic but not quite human; we see not the reflection of ourselves we had hoped for, but another thing looking back at us, watching us, situating us like Lacan's glittering can. The differential play that usually takes place along the axis between the viewer and the object is now internalized in the object itself and turned back on the viewer. Like the animals in a fable who speak with human voices, like Lacan's sardine can, Hejduk's objects stun us, inhumanly, with messages we sometimes wish we could suppress. Part of one's attraction to, but also dismay in the face of, the Masque characters is the incommensurable distance between the precision and fineness of the drawings—the clarity and efficiency with which they describe the geometry and tectonics of objects so controlled as to be almost cold, engineered, mechanical—and the depth and complexity of emotion they conjure. All of the literature on Hejduk's work points in some way to this latter effect. Some writers claim to be able to channel through his objects the most horrifying of modernity's forces. Others find joyous, almost comic enclosures to protect them or distract them from the same. Surely both are right. For what these otherwise opposing perceptions share is an existential uncertainty generated by the architecture itself: the recognition of the fact that our cultural identities, our very foundations, are outside ourselves, in the clusters of images and codes through which we are culturally apprehended. As with Lacan's gaze, which he once termed "the presence of others as such," so with Hejduk's Masques: in both we confront the fact that our subjectivity depends on the symbolic ratification of the Other.

When we recognize that we exist only by and for some Other, we may react with horror, but also, perhaps, with renewed ambition and determination. Jean-Paul Sartre's *Being and Nothingness* of 1943, from which Lacan draws his own meditations on the gaze, characterizes this decentering of the self in terms of an insistently Christian thematics: our self-definition, our dependency on the Other, is a lapse into a "fallen" state that is registered as a visual exchange between subject and object.[4] More than any other contemporary architect, Hejduk broods on our fall from grace, on the contradiction between fullness and loss, and how it can be figured, made palpable, in the experience of architecture. This is the same contradiction, I think, that Hejduk finds manifest in the architecture of Christ's cross. "What always interests me in the old paintings of the crucifixion is the construction of the cross. How the cross was constructed? How it was detailed? I think that it is important to know."[5] But, of course, it's not about construction alone. As well as being spatially and tectonically precise, the cross is the focus of the themes of individuality and collectivity, unspeakable loss and humbling plenitude, that Hejduk returns to again and again in his later work. The cross is the mark of the felt loss of architecture's original, divine mission of founding a promised land—a church on solid ground—and the necessary covering over of the site of that loss, masking it with architecture itself.[6] Somewhere among these attributes are suggestions to why Hejduk, in his last works, turned to an overtly religious imagery, but without swerving away from his experimentation with architecture's most basic elements and deepest structures. Perhaps it is the cross rather than the square or the diamond that is architecture's most primitive form. It is, no doubt, the most profound architectural element in Hejduk's terms of a double articulation of formal and tectonic development together with viewer-subject construction—the degree zero of the architectural sign. And it is under the sign of the cross that Hejduk brings his image-screen, his elevational chronotope, to its destination.

Hejduk's first steps toward that destination are intensely architectural, layering form upon form and manipulating them to a maximum. *Cathedral* is the most complex single object of Hejduk's career, gathering up the most significant of his formal inventions and collapsing them onto a simple rectangular volume, or perhaps a thick wall, with all the being-together of diverse formal elements on the vertical plane that his Wall apparatus captures. The original *Berlin Masque* building (which itself cannibalizes *Retreat Masque* and *Wall House 3*) operates as *Cathedral's* deep structure. Various other characters from *Berlin Masque* are there; *Wall House 3* reappears, now as one element of another wall; the *Collapse of Time* tower is on the roof; the various Morandi-like light cannons, funnels, and tubes that he experimented with in his architectural "Still Lifes" return, too.[7] It seems obvious that *Cathedral* is intended as a summation, and in this regard it is telling that just after the Canadian Centre for Architecture completed the *Cathedral* model, Hejduk began working on *A Gathering,* his unfinished site plan for a giant Masque (or perhaps it is an entire town) that was to contain the footprint of every project he had ever made. It is as if in these works Hejduk is cataloguing all the ways he has tried to arrest momentarily the unlocalizable architectural gaze.

But knowing Hejduk's penchant for binary conceptual organizations, is it not significant, too, that he was working on the series of thirty-two *Enclosures* at the same time? We know from correspondence that Hejduk considered *Enclosures* to be among the most important of his last works. Are they related in some way to *Cathedral*? Are *Enclosures* the absolute reduction and essentialization beyond which his architecture could not go? Accumulation is one way of making manifest the structures and codes that underlie perception, an end-of-the-line strategy in which an array of variations articulate the theme more precisely. The reuse, again and again, of *Wall House 3*—in *Cemetery for the Ashes of Thought,* in *Berlin Masque,* and its final return in *Cathedral*—is an example of this sort of pondering. But after the early Diamond Houses and Wall Houses, Hejduk tried to reach through this sort of complexity of accrual—the complexity that results from the piling up of form in *Cathedral* or *A Gathering*—to a place beyond the end of the line, where one might glimpse the foundations of formalization itself. And for that, synthesis and reduction are necessary—the kind of peeling away of form evident in *Enclosures* that seeks the matrix beneath. *Enclosures* can be placed in Hejduk's schema, chronologically and logically, as the second term of a binary that begins with the maximization of *Cathedral,* as the dialectical opposition along the same axis of summation and closure, the necessary complementary device for his endgame signification.

How are we to read *Enclosures*? In a set of drawings called *Sanctuary 3,* now held in The Menil Collection, and another for a project entitled *Chapel, Wedding of the Moon and Sun,* given by Hejduk to Charles Gwathmey, all made after *Cathedral* and *Christ Chapel* and probably just before *Enclosures,* are several sketches of sanctuaries and chapels, triangular in plan, with crucifixes suspended at various angles. "I desired the most simple structure for the space," writes Hejduk in his explanation of *Chapel* in a note on one of the drawings in Gwathmey's collection. And indeed, it is as if his early diagram of the space of the present has now found a final variant of its form, neither diamond nor wall, but the stage in between—a diamond in the process of flattening, a diamond becoming a wall:

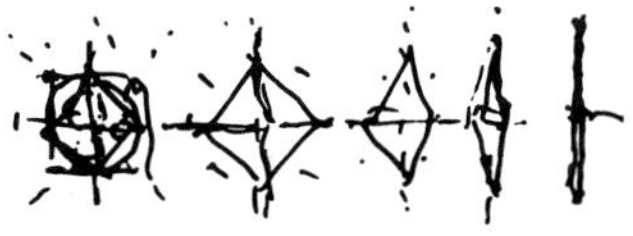

As did the diamond in plan and the wall in elevation, now the simple triangular space functions volumetrically to produce the dialectical relationship between depth and flatness. But the diagrams of this space resemble nothing so much as Lacan's diagram of the gaze, of vision turned back on itself. And the cross suspended in the triangular chapel, notwithstanding its clear and undeniable Christian meanings, functions also, I suggest, as a Wall-like apparatus, Lacan's *dompte regard,* an image-screen or mask that both focuses and tames the architectural gaze, mediates and puts into collectively recognizable form the sheer power of cumulative spatial experience. For this is not an ordinary Christian icon; rather, something is being done to the crucifix, and it is being done *architecturally* (just as in the Diamond Houses, the Wall Houses, and *The Collapse of Time*), by tilting planes in space, by setting up impossible orders (astronomic alignments, for example), by conflating incommensurable worlds, all of which challenge our optical-geometrical mastery of space and install us, as well, in the larger picture. Hejduk's crucifix is analogous to devices other artists have used when a powerful technique had to be brought to some sort of closure, to an absolute inwardness or, equally, to an absolute exteriority. Think, for example, of the *Last Supper* of Leonardo, where the vanishing point of the Renaissance's perspective system pierces the halo of Christ. Or the way Malevich hung his *Black Square* like an icon across the corner of the gallery in the *0,10* exhibition. Think of Le Corbusier's *Open Hand.* Or Robert Wilson's *14 Stations.* Religious imagery has historically provided art with the most widely understandable code for its attempts at transcending this unsatisfactory world or at proposing to put some other in its place. By the time of *Enclosures,* Hejduk's architecture had outgrown the formal system he had spent his life developing. He had to find a new device of signification to progress beyond it. Or, perhaps, an old one.

There is one reading of *Enclosures*, then, that is too literal but correct nonetheless. Each of the *Enclosures* portrays a scene that one might view in the deep triangular space of Hejduk's various sanctuaries, pressed onto a flattened plane located where the tilted crucifix otherwise would have been. In some of the *Enclosures*, in fact, the triangular plan is still there, tilted up vertically like a Cubist table. The *Enclosures* are the stained glass windows of the sanctuaries, the luminous membrane that separates worlds through encodings of a Real we cannot otherwise know. The *Enclosures* are the Wall, whose anthropomorphic building parts hovering in air have now become human: the spiky hair of the *Berlin Masque* creatures is now a crown of thorns, the V-shaped roofs have become angels' wings, the horned creatures of *Museum for War and Peace* have evolved into bulls. The actors are sandwiched and separated by thin registers, allowing angels and bulls, martyrs and mourners to slide past one another, while the architecture minimally frames their movements—invoking its pre-perspectival, narrative vocation in medieval painting, to provide the setting in which the action can be played out. The *Enclosures* are Hejduk's answer to Giotto's *Saint Francis* series, with its floating Christ, holy rays, and spewing stigmata. And to Le Corbusier, who wrote, "I have not experienced the miracle of faith but I have often known the miracle of inexpressible space."[8]

More precisely, the *Enclosures* are the image-screen first sought in the Diamond Houses and Wall Houses: the summation of architecture's history (from pre-perspectival space through Cubist space, up to the present), the inscription of otherness in the field of vision, the face that looks back at us, the mask and the masque that subdues and negotiates meanings and experiences too great for us to see directly. "The face crystallizes all redundancies, it emits and receives, releases and recaptures signifying signs. It is a whole body unto itself: it is like the body of the center of signifiance to which all of the deterritorialized signs affix themselves, and it marks the limit of their deterritorialization. . . . The face is what gives the signifier substance. . . . The mask does not hide the face, it *is* the face."[9] This passage is from Deleuze and Guattari's study of "faciality," the name given to the condition or production of a specific, though provisional, authorization and regulation of visual images out of a proliferation of signification and subjectification. And it could also describe Hejduk's last works. Like Hejduk's Wall apparatus, Deleuze and Guattari's faciality is conceived as a signifying surface: "Signifiance [the capacity for signification] is never without a white wall upon which it inscribes its signs and redundancies."[10] Faciality restricts the polyvocality of signs and the constructedness of subjects even as it draws on and retains some of their excessive potential. In Hejduk's case, the faciality of *Enclosures* was necessary to oppose and contain the limitless signification of *Cathedral*, necessary to overcome the entropy inherent in such an endlessly circulating formal system as his, with all its repetition and proliferation.

In his last works, Hejduk found himself facing a division, a contradiction between a dream of fullness and plenitude of experience, of depth and profundity of meaning, and a vision of the limits of what architecture can do, the lack built into its representational system. But of course this lack is but a reflection of the boundary of what it is humanly possible to perceive and the wish to cross over it. *Enclosures* mark the limit condition of architectural signification and coordinate an entire regime of loss and desired redemption, which the Christian imagery helps to represent. Deleuze and Guattari also put the face of Christ in the center of faciality's regime. Christ is the Western cultural gaze, the writer of codes, the standard against which variation and deviation are measured. And facialization is effected, at least in part, by stigmata, the trace of a limit condition. Faciality is the visible mark of pathos, but also the promise of getting beyond it (for did not the resurrected, transformed Christ admonish Thomas to probe the wound that had guaranteed humanity's salvation?). The *Enclosures* are the architectural stigmata on the corpus of Hejduk's work. They trace a certain failure or loss—the moment in which architecture glimpses its inadequacy—but hold out the possibility of new orders and perceptions. "This is the time for drawing angels," Hejduk insisted, the time for keeping that possibility always in sight.[11]

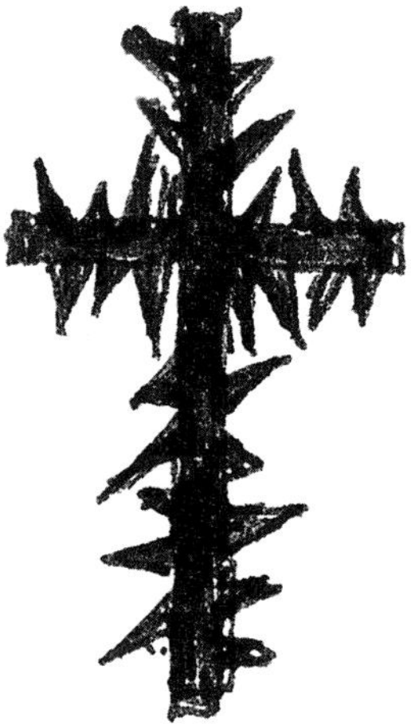

1. The highlighted numbers on each spread of this essay refer the reader to the images on the verso of the respective spreads of this book, illustrating and expanding the essay. Each of the thirty-two *Enclosures* appears on the recto in the order specified by Hejduk.

2. Walter Benjamin, "On Some Motifs in Baudelaire," in *Illuminations*, ed. Hannah Arendt, trans. Harry Zohn (New York: Harcourt, Brace, and World, 1968), 190.

3. Jacques Lacan, *The Four Fundamental Concepts of Psycho-Analysis*, ed. Jacques-Alain Miller, trans. Alan Sheridan (London: The Hogarth Press, 1977), 107. See "Of the Gaze As," in Lacan, for his explication of the gaze.

4. See Jean-Paul Sartre, "The Look," in *Being and Nothingness: An Essay in Phenomenological Ontology*, trans. Hazel E. Barnes (Secaucus, New Jersey: Citadel Press, 1956).

5. John Hejduk, "The Architect Who Drew Angels," interview by David Shapiro, *Architecture and Urbanism* no. 244 (January 1991), 59.

6. For a discussion of Hejduk's work as a peculiarly American quest for a promised land, see Catherine Ingraham, "Errand, Detour, and the Wilderness Urbanism of John Hejduk," in K. Michael Hays, ed., *Hejduk's Chronotope* (New York: Princeton Architectural Press in cooperation with the Canadian Centre for Architecture, Montreal, 1996).

7. What Hejduk called his "Still Lifes" are published in John Hejduk, *Adjusting Foundations*, ed. Kim Shkapich (New York: The Cooper Union for the Advancement of Science and Art in association with The Monacelli Press, 1995).

8. Le Corbusier, quoted in William J.R. Curtis, *Modern Architecture since 1900* (Englewood Cliffs, New Jersey: Prentice-Hall, 1983), 273.

9. Gilles Deleuze and Félix Guattari, "Year Zero: Faciality," in *A Thousand Plateaus*, trans. Brian Massumi (Minneapolis: University of Minnesota Press, 1987), 115. Deleuze and Guattari build on and "correct" Lacan and Sartre: "In the literature of the face, Sartre's text on the look and Lacan's on the mirror make the error of appealing to a form of subjectivity or humanity reflected in a phenomenological field or split in a structural field. *The gaze is but secondary in relation to the gazeless eyes, to the black hole of faciality. The mirror is but secondary in relation to the white wall of faciality.*" (171, Deleuze and Guattari's emphasis)

10. Deleuze and Guattari, 167.

11. Hejduk, "The Architect Who Drew Angels," 59.

ILLUSTRATIONS

Dimensions are in inches followed by centimeters; height precedes width.

An asterisk (*) denotes a work not included in the exhibition ***Sanctuaries: The Last Works of John Hejduk, Selections from the John Hejduk Archive at the Canadian Centre for Architecture, Montreal, and The Menil Collection, Houston*** at the Whitney Museum of American Art, New York, September 21, 2002–January 5, 2003, and at The Menil Collection, Houston, May 23–August 31, 2003.

Front cover:
Museum for War and Peace (M-09) [1 of 25 parts], 1999–2000
Pencil, ink, and gouache on Japanese kozo paper, 25 x 18 1/2 (63.5 x 47)
The Menil Collection, Houston; gift of the artist 2000-001.09
Photograph courtesy Estate of John Hejduk

Half-title page:
Details for Christ Chapel, from the book ***Pewter Wings, Golden Horns, Stone Veils***, 1996 (negative image)
Pen and black ink on wove paper, 11 x 8 1/2 (27.9 x 21.6)
John Hejduk Archive; Centre Canadien d'Architecture/Canadian Centre for Architecture, Montreal DR1998:0134:016:013

In "Illuminated Presence" by Toshiko Mori:
****Portrait of John Hejduk***
© 1985 Jose Pelaez, New York
Photograph courtesy Estate of John Hejduk

In this unpaginated volume, ***Enclosures***, a thirty-two-part suite, appears in sequence on the right-hand pages of each illustrated spread. Additional illustrations are referenced according to the ***Enclosures*** drawing on the opposite page, E-01 to E-32.

Enclosures [32 parts], 1999–2000
Ink and gouache on paper, 11 x 8 1/2 (27.9 x 21.6) each
The Menil Collection, Houston 2000-009.01-32
Photographs courtesy Estate of John Hejduk

Opposite E-02:
Berlin Masque, 1981
Painted wood, 9 x 36 1/8 x 36 3/16 (23 x 92.7 x 92.8)
John Hejduk Archive; Centre Canadien d'Architecture/Canadian Centre for Architecture, Montreal DR1998:0098:007
Photograph courtesy Estate of John Hejduk

Opposite E-03:
Wall House 3, 1974
Painted wood, 7 7/16 x 9 1/16 x 28 1/8 (19 x 23.3 x 72.1)
John Hejduk Archive; Centre Canadien d'Architecture/Canadian Centre for Architecture, Montreal DR1998:0079:040

Opposite E-04:
Cathedral, 1996 (detail)
Painted wood, 24 x 48 x 17 (61 x 121.9 x 43.2)
John Hejduk Archive; Centre Canadien d'Architecture/Canadian Centre for Architecture, Montreal DR1998:0134:014 (view 1)

Opposite E-05:
Top: ***The Red Cube, "Blood from Paul Celan,"*** 1999–2000
Watercolor on tracing paper with tape, 18 1/2 x 26 1/2 (47 x 67.3)
Private collection
Photograph courtesy Estate of John Hejduk

Bottom: ***The Red Cube, "Blood from Paul Celan,"*** 1999–2000
Watercolor on tracing paper, 25 1/8 x 38 1/8 (63.8 x 97.8)
Private collection
Photograph courtesy Estate of John Hejduk

Opposite E-06:
****Diamond Museum C***, 1962–67 (reproduced from ***Mask of Medusa: Works, 1947–1983***, p. 251)
John Hejduk Archive;
Photograph courtesy Estate of John Hejduk

Opposite E-07:
Top: ***Museum for War and Peace (M-13) [1 of 25 parts]***, 1999–2000
Pencil, ink, and gouache on Japanese kozo paper, 25 x 38 3/4 (63.5 x 98.4)
The Menil Collection, Houston; gift of the artist 2000-001.13
Photograph courtesy Estate of John Hejduk

Bottom: ****Museum for War and Peace (M-04) [1 of 25 parts]***, 1999–2000
Ink and gouache on paper, 6 3/8 x 9 (16.2 x 22.9)
The Menil Collection, Houston; gift of the artist 2000-001.04
Photograph courtesy Estate of John Hejduk

Opposite E-08:
Andalusian Wall Houses (1 of 24), 1995
Ink and watercolor on paper, 11 x 8 1/2 (27.9 x 21.6)
Private collection
Photograph courtesy Estate of John Hejduk

Opposite E-09:
Sanctuary 1 (1-13) [1 of 17 parts], 1999–2000
Ink and gouache on paper, 11 x 8 1/2 (27.9 x 21.6)
The Menil Collection, Houston; gift of the artist 2000-002.13
Photograph courtesy Estate of John Hejduk

Opposite E-10:
Christ Chapel, 1996 (detail)
Painted wood, 13 5/8 x 29 13/16 x 39 7/8 (35 x 76.5 x 102.3)
John Hejduk Archive; Centre Canadien d'Architecture/Canadian Centre for Architecture, Montreal DR1998:0134:016 (view 4)

Opposite E-11:
Christ Chapel, 1996 (detail)
Painted wood, 13 5/8 x 29 13/16 x 39 7/8 (35 x 76.5 x 102.3)
John Hejduk Archive; Centre Canadien d'Architecture/Canadian Centre for Architecture, Montreal DR1998:0134:016 (view 1)

Opposite E-12:
Interior Perspective for Christ Chapel, from the book ***Pewter Wings, Golden Horns, Stone Veils***, 1996 (negative image)
Pen and black ink on wove paper, 11 x 8 1/2 (27.9 x 21.6)
John Hejduk Archive; Centre Canadien d'Architecture/Canadian Centre for Architecture, Montreal DR1998:0134:016:003

Opposite E-13:
Cathedral, 1996
Painted wood, 24 x 48 x 17 (61 x 121.9 x 43.2)
John Hejduk Archive; Centre Canadien d'Architecture/Canadian Centre for Architecture, Montreal DR1998:0134:014 (view 7)

Opposite E-14:
Cathedral, 1996
Painted wood, 24 x 48 x 17 (61 x 121.9 x 43.2)
John Hejduk Archive; Centre Canadien d'Architecture/Canadian Centre for Architecture, Montreal DR1998:0134:014 (view 8)

Opposite E-15:
Cathedral, 1996 (detail)
Painted wood, 24 x 48 x 17 (61 x 121.9 x 43.2)
John Hejduk Archive; Centre Canadien d'Architecture/Canadian Centre for Architecture, Montreal DR1998:0134:014 (view 3)

Opposite E-16:
Cathedral, 1996 (detail)
Painted wood, 24 x 48 x 17 (61 x 121.9 x 43.2)
John Hejduk Archive; Centre Canadien d'Architecture/Canadian Centre for Architecture, Montreal DR1998:0134:014 (view 10)

Opposite E-17:
Cathedral, 1996 (detail)
Painted wood, 24 x 48 x 17 (61 x 121.9 x 43.2)
John Hejduk Archive; Centre Canadien d'Architecture/Canadian Centre for Architecture, Montreal DR1998:0134:014 (view 9)

Opposite E-18:
Perspective for Cathedral, from the book ***Pewter Wings, Golden Horns, Stone Veils***, 1996
Black ink on wove paper, 11 x 8 1/2 (27.9 x 21.6)
John Hejduk Archive; Centre Canadien d'Architecture/Canadian Centre for Architecture, Montreal DR1998:0134:014:007

Opposite E-19:
Cathedral, 1996
Painted wood, 24 x 48 x 17 (61 x 121.9 x 43.2)
John Hejduk Archive; Centre Canadien d'Architecture/Canadian Centre for Architecture, Montreal DR1998:0134:014 (view 6)

Opposite E-20:
Cathedral, 1996 (detail)
Painted wood, 24 x 48 x 17 (61 x 121.9 x 43.2)
John Hejduk Archive; Centre Canadien d'Architecture/Canadian Centre for Architecture, Montreal DR1998:0134:014 (view 11)

Opposite E-21:
Bird's-Eye View of Structures Overlooking Cathedral Site and a Postcard Painting of the Annunciation, from the sketchbook ***Pewter Wings—Cathedral***, 1996
Pen, black ink, watercolor, and collage element on wove paper, 11 x 8 1/2 (27.9 x 21.6) each
John Hejduk Archive; Centre Canadien d'Architecture/Canadian Centre for Architecture, Montreal DR1998:0134:014:001-053

Opposite E-22:
Site Plan for A Gathering, 1999 (detail of installation of twelve drawings)
Ink and gouache on paper, 34 x 33 (86.4 x 83.8) overall
Private collection
Photograph courtesy Estate of John Hejduk

Opposite E-23:
Site Plan for A Gathering, 1999 (installation of twelve drawings)
Ink and gouache on paper, 34 x 33 (86.4 x 83.8) overall
Private collection
Photograph courtesy Estate of John Hejduk

Opposite E-24:
Chapel, Wedding of the Moon and Sun, 1998
Ink on paper, 9 x 8 7/16 (22.9 x 21.4)
Collection of Charles Gwathmey
Photograph courtesy Estate of John Hejduk

Opposite E-25:
Chapel, Wedding of the Moon and Sun, 1998
Ink on paper, 8 1/2 x 11 (21.6 x 27.9)
Collection of Charles Gwathmey
Photograph courtesy Estate of John Hejduk

Opposite E-26:
Sanctuary 1 (1-02) [1 of 17 parts], 1999–2000
Ink and gouache on paper, 11 x 8 1/2 (27.9 x 21.6)
The Menil Collection, Houston; gift of the artist 2000-002.02
Photograph courtesy Estate of John Hejduk

Opposite E-27:
Sanctuary 1 (1-03) [1 of 17 parts], 1999–2000
Ink and gouache on paper, 11 x 8 1/2 (27.9 x 21.6)
The Menil Collection, Houston; gift of the artist 2000-002.03
Photograph courtesy Estate of John Hejduk

Opposite E-28:
***Sanctuary 1 (1-09) [1 of 17 parts]**, 1999–2000
Ink and gouache on paper, 11 x 8 1/2 (27.9 x 21.6)
The Menil Collection, Houston; gift of the artist 2000-002.09
Photograph courtesy Estate of John Hejduk

Opposite E-29:
***House of the Suicide** and **House of the Mother of the Suicide**, 1991
(installation view of Royal Gardens, Prague Castle)
Photograph by Hélène Binet, courtesy Estate of John Hejduk

Opposite E-30:
Sanctuary 3 (3-08) [1 of 16 parts], 1999–2000 (detail)
Ink, gouache, and collage element on paper, 11 x 8 1/2 (27.9 x 21.6)
The Menil Collection, Houston; gift of the artist 2000-004.08
Photograph courtesy Estate of John Hejduk

Opposite E-31:
***Sanctuary 3 (3-11) [1 of 16 parts]**, 1999–2000 (detail)
Ink on letterhead with collage elements, 11 x 8 1/2 (27.9 x 21.6)
The Menil Collection, Houston; gift of the artist 2000-004.11
Photograph courtesy Estate of John Hejduk

Opposite E-32:
Sanctuary 3 (3-15) [1 of 16 parts], 1999–2000 (detail)
Ink, gouache, and collage elements on letterhead, 16 13/16 x 8 1/2 (42.7 x 21.6)
The Menil Collection, Houston; gift of the artist 2000-004.15
Photograph by Hester + Hardaway, Houston

In "Architecture's Destiny" by K. Michael Hays:
On title page (left) and throughout text:
Diamond Museum C, 1962–67 (details; see illustration opposite E-06)

Opposite title page:
Cathedral, 1996 (detail; see illustration opposite E-19)

Back cover:
Sanctuary 2 (2-07) [1 of 9 parts], 1999–2000 (detail)
Ink on letterhead with collage elements, 11 x 8 1/2 (27.9 x 21.6)
The Menil Collection, Houston; gift of the artist 2000-003.7
Photograph courtesy Estate of John Hejduk

SELECTED BIBLIOGRAPHY

BOOKS AND EXHIBITION CATALOGUES BY JOHN HEJDUK

Adjusting Foundations. Edited by Kim Shkapich. New York: The Cooper Union for the Advancement of Science and Art in association with The Monacelli Press, 1995.

Aesop's Fables. Told by Joseph Jacobs. Illustrated by John Hejduk. New York: Rizzoli International Publications, 1991.

Architectures in Love: Sketchbook Notes. New York: Rizzoli International Publications, 1995.

Berlin Night (exhibition catalogue). Rotterdam: Netherlands Architecture Institute, 1993.

The Black Swan. By Thomas Mann. Lithographs by John Hejduk. New York: The Limited Editions Club, 1990.

Bovisa (exhibition catalogue). Edited by José Rafael Moneo. Cambridge, Massachusetts: Harvard University Graduate School of Design; New York: Rizzoli International Publications, 1987.

The Collapse of Time and Other Diary Constructions (exhibition catalogue). With writing by David Shapiro and a photograph essay by Hélène Binet. London: The Architectural Association, 1987.

Fabrications, John Hejduk. New York: The Cooper Union for the Advancement of Science and Art, 1974.

John Hejduk: Riga. Ausstellung vom 16. Juni bis 9. Juli 1988 (exhibition catalogue). Berlin: Aedes Galerie für Architektur und Raum, 1988.

John Hejduk: 7 Houses. January 22–February 16, 1980 (exhibition catalogue). New York: The Institute for Architecture and Urban Studies, 1980.

John Hejduk: The Riga Project. November 20–December 22, 1987 (exhibition catalogue). Philadelphia: The University of the Arts, The Rosenwald-Wolf Gallery and The Great Hall, 1989.

The Lancaster/Hanover Masque = Le masque Lancaster/Hanover (exhibition catalogue). With writing by Wim van den Bergh. London: Architectural Association; Montreal: Centre Canadien d'Architecture/Canadian Centre for Architecture, 1992.

Lines: No Fire Could Burn. New York: The Monacelli Press, 1999.

Mask of Medusa: Works, 1947–1983. Edited by Kim Shkapich. New York: Rizzoli International Publications, 1985.

Pewter Wings, Golden Horns, Stone Veils: Wedding in a Dark Plum Room. Edited by Kim Shkapich. Montreal: Canadian Centre for Architecture in cooperation with The Monacelli Press, New York, 1997.

Projects/John Hejduk, Architect (exhibition catalogue). Paris: Fondation Le Corbusier, 1972.

Riga, Vladivostok, Lake Baikal. Edited by Kim Shkapich. New York: Rizzoli International Publications, 1989.

The Silent Witnesses and Other Poems. New York: The Institute for Architecture and Urban Studies, 1980.

Soundings. Edited by Kim Shkapich. New York: Rizzoli International Publications, 1993.

Such Places as Memory: Poems, 1953–1996. Cambridge, Massachusetts: The MIT Press, 1998.

Three Projects (exhibition catalogue). New York: The Cooper Union School of Art and Architecture in cooperation with The Architectural League of New York and The Graham Foundation for Advanced Studies in the Fine Arts, 1969.

Victims (exhibition catalogue). London: Architectural Association, 1986.

BOOKS AND EXHIBITION CATALOGUES ON JOHN HEJDUK

Flores, Ricardo, and Eva Prats, eds. ***John Hejduk: House for a Poet*** (exhibition catalogue). Barcelona: Edicions UPC, 2000.

Hays, K. Michael, ed. ***Hejduk's Chronotope***. With writings by Stan Allen, Peggy Deamer, Catherine Ingraham, Detlef Mertins, Edward Mitchell, and R.E. Somol. New York: Princeton Architectural Press in cooperation with the Canadian Centre for Architecture, Montreal, 1996.

Thån, Astri, ed. ***Security***. With writings by Sverre Fehn, John Hejduk, and David Shapiro, and photo essays by Annette Faltin and Hélène Binet. Oslo: Aventura Forlag, 1995.

van de Wal, Olof, and Anne Wolff, eds. ***Wall House #2: John Hejduk in Groningen***. Groningen, Netherlands: Platform Gras, 2001.

ACKNOWLEDGMENTS

In 2000 Maxwell L. Anderson, Alice Pratt Brown Director of the Whitney Museum of American Art, and the Museum launched a program to exhibit and acquire significant works of architecture and to generally support the development and dissemination of architectural knowledge. The exhibition *Sanctuaries: The Last Works of John Hejduk, Selections from the John Hejduk Archive at the Canadian Centre for Architecture, Montreal, and The Menil Collection, Houston* and the present volume are among the first fruits of the Whitney's architecture initiative. Max Anderson has generously supported this project in every way.

I never met John Hejduk, the man, unfortunately—the big bear from the Bronx who inspired and is loved by so many—but to the work of Hejduk, the architect, I have devoted much attention in my roles as scholar and teacher. It was in discussions with Toshiko Mori—discussions about architecture's recent past, its present moment, and the role of the Whitney architecture program in the larger scene—that I first became convinced of the rightness of Hejduk as the subject for my first exhibition at the Whitney. Along with Toshiko, Susan de Menil helped me understand the full promise of giving focus to this work at this time. I have greatly benefited from their advice and friendship.

Among the many members of the Whitney staff who helped with the Hejduk project, I am particularly grateful to Christy Putnam, associate director for exhibitions and collections management, for guiding me through the myriad doors of a first-time exhibition; and to Meg Calvert, coordinator, exhibitions and collections management, for her enthusiastic and tireless assistance in every aspect of the exhibition and catalogue. In the Department of Registration, special thanks to Suzanne Quigley, head registrar, for her determination to install the impossibly large structures in the Sculpture Court; and to Kelley Loftus, assistant paper preparator, for her thoughtfulness and care. I have learned much about the curatorial craft from Maura Heffner, assistant curator and manager, Touring Exhibitions Program.

Garrett White, director of the Department of Publications and New Media, and Rachel Wixom, managing editor, pushed this publication through an impossible schedule with skill and grace. Thanks to Garrett, Meg Calvert, Thea Hetzner, assistant editor, Libby Hruska, assistant editor, and Kari Steeves, consultant, interpretive materials, for their advice on the catalogue essay and exhibition texts, and to Makiko Ushiba, senior graphic designer, and Mark Steigelman, manager, design and construction, for their advice on design.

Working with Kim Shkapich on her design of this book has been an absolute pleasure.

The publication would not have been possible without a gift from the Harvard Design School, Cambridge, and gifts from John Jay Iselin and Josephine Lea Iselin; Irma Giustino Weiss; the Menil Foundation, Inc., Houston; the Iselin Fund at Berkshire Taconic Community Foundation; and the Josiah Macy Jr. Foundation.

This publication would also never have been realized without the dedication of Toshiko Mori, chair of the Department of Architecture, Harvard University Graduate School of Design, and Peter Rowe, dean. Their commitment to architecture's intellectual project and their generosity of spirit has exceeded even high expectations.

I am grateful to the Canadian Centre for Architecture, Montreal; The Menil Collection, Houston; and the other institutions and individuals who loaned works from their collection. Thomas Galloway, dean of the College of Architecture, Georgia Institute of Technology, Atlanta; and Ellen Dunham-Jones, chair of the Department of Architecture, facilitated the donation of the *House of the Suicide* and the *House of the Mother of the Suicide*, the two large structures that had been originally constructed by James Williamson and students at Georgia Tech at the College of Architecture. For Jim, "the resurrection," as we called it—the removal of the pieces of these structures from a storage basement in Atlanta and their installation at the Whitney—was a labor of love and dedication. My sincere appreciation goes to him.

Anthony Vidler, dean of the Irwin S. Chanin School of Architecture at The Cooper Union, and Steven Hillyer, director of the School of Architecture archive, generously made possible the construction of the model *Chapel, Wedding of the Moon and Sun*. Alexandra Kiss, Michael LaFreniere, and Amir Shahrokhi of the Internship Program of The Cooper Union built the model under Steven's direction.

In my attempts to understand the last works of John Hejduk, my greatest joy has come through discussions of the work with Renata Hejduk, Howard Shubert, and Kim Shkapich. Howard and Kim could easily claim to have been co-curators of the exhibition. Howard and I spent hours in the vaults of the Canadian Centre for Architecture pondering and sorting the drawings. During the intense moments of selection, I talked with Kim almost every day. It was not until, after several trials, she smiled silently at my sketch of the exhibition that I knew I had gotten it right.

K. Michael Hays

Adjunct Curator of Architecture, Whitney Museum of American Art
Eliot Noyes Professor of Architectural Theory,
Harvard University Graduate School of Design

COLOPHON

This book was published in association with the Harvard Design School in conjunction with the exhibition *Sanctuaries: The Last Works of John Hejduk, Selections from the John Hejduk Archive at the Canadian Centre for Architecture, Montreal, and The Menil Collection, Houston* at the Whitney Museum of American Art, New York, September 21, 2002–January 5, 2003, and at The Menil Collection, Houston, May 23–August 31, 2003.

Support for this exhibition is provided by the Director's Council of the Whitney Museum of American Art.

A portion of the proceeds from the sale of this book benefits The John Hejduk Soundings Fellowship and the Whitney Museum of American Art and its programs.

Sanctuaries: The Last Works of John Hejduk, Selections from the John Hejduk Archive at the Canadian Centre for Architecture, Montreal, and The Menil Collection, Houston was organized by K. Michael Hays, adjunct curator of architecture, Whitney Museum of American Art, with the assistance of Meg Calvert, coordinator, exhibitions and collections management.

This publication was produced by the Publications and New Media Department at the Whitney Museum of American Art: Garrett White, director of publications and new media; Rachel de W. Wixom, managing editor; Thea Hetzner, assistant editor; Libby Hruska, assistant editor; Makiko Ushiba, senior graphic designer; Christine Knorr, graphic designer; Vickie Leung, production manager; Anita Duquette, manager, rights and reproductions; Jennifer Belt, photographs and permissions coordinator; Carolyn Ramo, publications and new media assistant.

Text editors: Garrett White, Thea Hetzner, Libby Hruska

Proofreader: David E. Brown

Catalogue design: Kim Shkapich

Printed in Germany by Cantz
Bound by Bramscher Buchbinder Betriebe, Bramsche, Germany
Color separations: C+S Repro, Filderstadt, Germany

LIBRARY OF CONGRESS CATALOGING-IN-PUBLICATION DATA

Hays, K. Michael.
Sanctuaries, the last works of John Hejduk : selections from the John Hejduk Archive at the Canadian Centre for Architecture, Montreal, and The Menil Collection, Houston / K. Michael Hays ; preface by Toshiko Mori.
p. cm.
ISBN 0-87427-129-0
1. Hejduk, John, 1929---Exhibitions. 2. Architecture--United States--20th century-- Exhibitions. I. Title: Sanctuaries. II. Title: Last works of John Hejduk. III. Hejduk, John, 1929- IV. Title.
NA737.H46 A4 2002
720'.92--dc21
2002011435

945 Madison Avenue at 75th Street
New York, NY 10021
www.whitney.org

Distributed in 2002 by

ABRAMS

Harry N. Abrams, Inc.
100 Fifth Avenue
New York, NY 10011
www.abramsbooks.com

Abrams is a subsidiary of

LA MARTINIÈRE GROUPE

Printed in Germany